YOU HAVE THE POWER

How to Take Back Our Country and
Restore Democracy in America

HOWARD DEAN
with Judith Warner

Simon & Schuster Paperbacks
New York London Toronto Sydney

SIMON & SCHUSTER PAPERBACKS
Rockefeller Center
1230 Avenue of the Americas
New York, NY 10020

First Simon & Schuster paperback edition 2006

SIMON & SCHUSTER PAPERBACKS and colophon are registered trademarks
of Simon & Schuster, Inc.

For information about special discounts for bulk purchases,
please contact Simon & Schuster Special Sales at
1-800-456-6798 or business@simonandschuster.com

Designed by Helene Berinsky

Manufactured in the United States of America

1   3   5   7   9   10   8   6   4   2

Library of Congress Cataloging-in-Publication Data is available.

ISBN-13: 978-0-7432-7013-7
ISBN-10:   0-7432-7013-4
ISBN-13: 978-0-7432-9149-1 (Pbk)
ISBN-10:   0-7432-9149-2 (Pbk)

To the incredibly patriotic Americans of all ages who worked so hard during my campaign to bring America back on track;

To my mother, Andree, and my brothers, Jim and Bill, who became leaders in their own right;

And to Judy, Anne, and Paul, who sustain me through every adventure and through every hardship.

Thank you.

ACKNOWLEDGMENTS

This book could not have been written without the hard work and exceptional writing and editing skills of Judy Warner. Her patience, persistence, and intelligence made this book what it is.

I want to thank Bob Barnett and Roy Neel for putting together the team that created this, and Geoff Kloske and David Rosenthal of Simon & Schuster for their insight and patience.

I'm grateful to Karen Hicks, Kate O'Connor, Mike O'Mary, and Joe Trippi for their willingness to participate in the creation of both the book and the vision that made the campaign work.

I thank Naric Rome, Alison Stanton, Chris Canning, Adam Michaelson, Tom McMahon, and Laura Gross for their help with the research required and I appreciate Jeff Nussbaum's help in updating this paperback edition.

Finally, I thank my wife, Judy Dean, for applying her usual common sense to my efforts. She made this book better reflect the incredible influence that all the people whom we met across America had on our lives during the past two years.

CONTENTS

PREFACE: FROM DFA TO THE DNC

Election Days are always tense affairs, and Tuesday, November 2, 2004, was no different. I had ended my own campaign for the presidency nine months earlier, but in the weeks that followed, I had devoted myself to barnstorming the country on behalf of John Kerry and scores of other candidates who shared our vision for a fiscally responsible, socially progressive America.

I've been through several Election Days when my own name was on the ballot, and once the voting begins, there's a feeling of powerlessness—you've done all you can do, and now it is in the hands of others. Even with the radio interviews and get-out-the-vote calls I was making, this day felt the same way, especially given that I had early-voted in Burlington the week before.

I settled into my office at Democracy for America, the grassroots organization that had grown out of the Dean for America campaign, and began engaging in gossip that runs rampant every Election Day. "What are you hearing?" "Record turnout in Philadelphia?" "Some irregularities in Ohio?" "Long lines at the polls in southern Florida." From these disparate tea leaves, you try to divine the mood of 120 million voters and get a sense of what things will look like when the polls close.

By two P.M., we had our first real information—preliminary exit polling information from the battleground states. Exit polling data comes from the National Election Pool, a consortium of television networks and the Associated Press, and the information is distributed to those sources and other paid subscribers, all of whom have pledged not to divulge it or discuss it until polls have closed.

Inevitably, the data leaks out, and when it got into our hands, this was what we saw:

Kerry, up by one in Florida. Up by one in Ohio. Up by nine in Pennsylvania. Up by five in Wisconsin. Up by four in Michigan. Up huge in Minnesota. Down two in Nevada. Up two in New Mexico. Down two in North Carolina. Up seven in Colorado.

If these numbers held up, and that was a big "if," we were looking at a landslide.

News outlets were seeing these numbers, too. Though experience has taught us that exit polls are not to be trusted entirely, news organizations still use early exit polls to get an idea which way their coverage is going to go later.

Several news outlets, feeling that John Kerry was on the verge of unseating George W. Bush, wanted to talk to me about my feelings concerning the election, what I thought I had contributed and what it would mean for America. I agreed to go on NBC News, which sent a private jet to fly me down from Burlington to their New York studios.

On the flight, Tom McMahon, the executive director of Democracy for America, Laura Gross, my communications director, and I began playing the quintessential political parlor game, asking ourselves, if Kerry won, who would he nominate to be in his cabinet? Would he ask me? Would he tackle the issue of health care—one of my signature campaign issues—right away?

After we had landed at Teterboro Airport and were waiting for a car to take us into Manhattan, a flight attendant from another plane came up to me and asked how things were looking.

"Good. Really, really good," I replied.

She handed me a bottle of champagne that I imagine was left over from one of her flights. "This is for later."

I thanked her and held the bottle of champagne. I don't drink, but I felt like we might be able to put it to good use.

In the car on the way to the studio, I called my family and told them things were looking up. By the time we got to the city, we were seeing four P.M. exit polling numbers, which looked as good as, if not better than, those we had seen earlier. I called my family members again to tell them what we were hearing. At NBC's studios, I did a whirlwind series of interviews. I talked about the campaign, and about how I felt the election would be a referendum on President Bush's leadership on both foreign policy and the economy. I couldn't help mentioning that things were looking good for Kerry.

However, as the evening wore on and polls closed across America and the vote count (rather than exit polls) started to come in, things began to look not nearly as good for Democrats across the country.

Florida, Ohio, and Iowa started trending toward Bush. By about eleven P.M., the folks at NBC told me they wouldn't need my commentary anymore. They didn't need someone to talk about the reemergence of the Democratic Party. It wasn't looking like we had reemerged.

Rather than fly home right away, I decided to swing by a party being sponsored by Democracy for New York and several other progressive organizations. I tried to stay upbeat for them, telling them that we were still waiting for results from Ohio, and congratulating them on the work they had done to ensure what would later prove to be a record Democratic turnout. But reality was beginning to settle in.

The flight home was much more subdued. I sat and reflected on all that had happened in the past year: A campaign that was, to many, a quixotic quest when it began had grown into a national movement, one that continued after my own campaign ended. I talked with Tom about what would be next for Democracy for America—the organization that had grown out of my campaign. I thought about what would be next for me.

When we got off the plane, we learned that Ohio had been called for Bush. I dropped Tom and Laura off at the office and headed home.

The next morning, back at the DFA headquarters, people were telling me that there had been voting irregularities in Ohio and elsewhere. They bucked me up by showing me that several members of the "Dean Dozen"—progressive candidates our organization supported outside of traditionally Democratic areas—had won. Still, we had lost the main event.

The days after the election brought a series of predictable recriminations: Where had Democrats gone wrong? What if John Kerry had run a different campaign? Immediately, some people began saying that in order to win, the Democratic Party needed to move more to the center—that we needed to be more like Republicans. Equally vocal were those who felt that the election had been decided on the issue of moral values.

I felt that we had tried being "Republican-lite," and it didn't work at all. My experience on the campaign trail and the victories I was seeing from some of the Dean Dozen candidates showed that people in so-called red states were hungry for an alternative, and hungry for candidates who were willing to stand up for their beliefs. Over fifty years ago, Harry Truman said of the Democratic Party, "We are not going to get anywhere by trimming or appeasing. And we don't need to try it."

As for the issue of moral values, I thought we were letting one question in an exit poll drive the entire Democratic Party into a panic. After all, the American people are more in agreement with our definition of moral values than they are with the persistent Republican invasion of personal privacy.

Beyond that, we seem to have forgotten somewhere that it is a moral value to provide health care. It is a moral value to educate our young people. The sense of community that comes from full participation in our democracy is a moral value. It is a moral value to make sure that we do not leave our own debts to be paid by the next generation. Honesty is a moral value. And yet these values appear to be absent in today's Republican establishment. Instead, they stand for little more than deficits, divisiveness, and deceit. We didn't need to change our values. We needed to start standing up for them.

Even before the election, I had talked sporadically with friends, family, and advisers about what would be next for me if John Kerry didn't win. One of the possibilities that kept coming up was my running for the chairmanship of the Democratic National Committee. At the time, my reaction was "absolutely not."

As a governor, I had seen the DNC as little more than an organization dedicated to electing a president, one that had long neglected cultivating the state and local candidates who would form the foundation of a strong party for generations to come. When I was a candidate for president, my interaction with the DNC was even more frustrating—it seemed like a bastion of Washington-based consultants who had no interest in hearing what I was saying, much less supporting what I was doing. Did I really want to lead a party that I loved but had been at war with for over a year?

Besides that, there was a lot of resistance within Democracy for America to my even thinking about running for DNC chair. A lot of our followers didn't consider themselves Democrats or have any particular love for the establishment of the Democratic Party.

Finally, I felt that the Democratic Party needed the type of overhaul that couldn't be accomplished from the top down, no matter who was at the top.

I had friends—both among DFA supporters and within the labor movement—who wanted me to consider starting a third party. They noted that my campaign had been a movement that went far beyond me; after my campaign ended, Dean for America supporters had set up Democracy for America organizations in just about every state. These people were active, energized, and ready to bring about real change in American politics. Again, I looked to them for leadership.

What I saw was that instead of abandoning the Democratic Party, DFA members began working *within* the Democratic Party to bring the bottom-up change that I had been talking about.

The first time I saw this was on a trip to northern California, where, along with Congresswoman Zoe Lofgren, I met with several DFA California activists. They told me that they had been going to California Democratic Party meetings and getting resolutions passed. I hate to say it, but I initially threw a bit of cold water on their work. I told them not to waste their time on internal fights. They didn't listen to me, and I'm glad they didn't. California's Democratic Party is organized by assembly districts, and in late December, the California for Democracy activists were elected as leaders in nearly fifty of them.

In Kentucky, where Democrats now hold the lowest level of public office leadership since 1955, Change for Kentucky sought to revitalize and reenergize the leadership of the state Democratic Party, and got over 250 "Dean Democrat" precinct leaders elected statewide.

In Maryland, Terry Lierman, one of my national campaign-finance chairs, ran for state party chair. Despite meager support from the Democratic establishment, he won.

In Oregon, Jenny Greenleaf, a DFA activist in Portland, knocked off a twelve-year incumbent to win election as a DNC member.

These victories weren't being organized from our headquarters in Burlington. They were happening because activists and organizers wanted to change the Democratic Party—and then use the Democratic Party to change politics in America.

In many ways, the movement wasn't ideological so much as it was practical. These people were trying to move the Democratic Party back to the organizational model that had worked for us in the past, but that we had abandoned in the era of soft money.

As I watched what was happening in state party after state party, I realized there was no way I could indulge thoughts of leading a third party when the people whose ideas I trusted and whose energy I relied on were working within the system to strengthen the Democratic Party. If these activists were really bringing about change in the Democratic Party from the grass roots up, it might just be possible for me to help them by working to change the party from the top down.

I began to rethink my decision not to seek the chairmanship of the Democratic Party.

Of course, the more I thought about it, the more I saw that I had no idea how one went about running for DNC chair. I began talking to folks who had been through it. Most notably, I sought the advice of veterans of Ron Brown's 1988 campaign for DNC chair.

Ron had run for DNC chair as an outsider who many thought was too liberal, but he came in and built the foundation for President Clinton's victories in 1992 and 1996.

There were some parallels between his race and the one I was considering, and the fact that Ron's widow, Alma, supported me firmed my resolve to try.

Running to lead the Democratic National Committee, I quickly learned, means running a campaign that is focused on the votes of 447 people. The DNC is perceived, somewhat incorrectly, as an establishment group. In actuality, it's a pretty good microcosm of the party as a whole—there are some insiders and some outsiders. It also includes a lot of folks hungry for change and even hungrier to win.

I started calling around and began finding that even though most people felt my campaign for president had been divisive, they were grateful for my work on behalf of John Kerry and John Edwards after the primaries.

On December 8, I went to George Washington University to give a speech about the future of the Democratic Party. I wanted to answer what had become the two prevailing schools of thought on our electoral losses: that we would need to move to the center, and that we would need to retake the issue of values. I told the assembled crowd, "There's only one thing Republican power brokers want more than for us to lurch to the left, and that's for us to lurch to the right. What they fear most is that we may really begin fighting for what we believe—the fiscally responsible, socially progressive values for which Democrats have always stood and fought."

I still hadn't decided whether to run for chair, but my

speech was a clear statement about the course I intended to set should I be elected DNC chair.

The next day I attended a meeting of the Association of State Party Chairs in Florida, and the message I delivered there was largely the same.

A few days later, I was at a similar meeting in Atlanta. One participant asked me, "What is your southern strategy?"

Without thinking, I responded, "Show up." I told him that we couldn't win races we didn't run. We needed to stop writing off entire regions, start running fifty-state campaigns, and start putting up candidates for every office. The more I talked about what we needed to do, the more excited I became about the prospect of doing it.

On January 11, I sent out an e-mail to my DFA membership announcing my decision. The subject line said simply, "I'm running."

We decided to take my campaign directly to the DNC members. I spent days on the phone, talking to members all across the country. On weekends, I went to different states to meet with members. I sent personalized letters to all 447 members. I told anyone I didn't know that I looked forward to meeting them. In a lot of the envelopes, I tossed in a copy of this book, or a DVD of my GWU speech and an appearance on *Meet the Press*.

After I had written to them, I called them. I just started going through the list alphabetically. I began every phone conversation: "Hi, it's Howard Dean calling." One woman in Nevada actually thought she was getting a robotic, pretaped call. It took a minute to convince her that it wasn't.

The resistance to my candidacy once again came from Beltway insiders, who said that my election would signal a leftward lurch in the party, that we'd be permanently relinquishing the South. But those claims were rebuffed from some of my earliest—and bravest—supporters. For example, Chairman Scott Maddox, Vice Chair Diane Glasser, and the entire Florida DNC membership unanimously endorsed me early in my campaign. Former congressman Wayne Dowdy, the chair of the Mississippi Democratic Party, did the same. Jay Parmley, the state chair in Oklahoma, endorsed me as well. Jay in particular took some heat for standing with me. But collectively, they demonstrated that my message of "show up" was resonating, and that Democrats throughout America were looking for change.

Meanwhile, the calls were going well. Other candidates in the race began to drop out. Everyone I talked to just wanted to win. They thought it would be good to shake things up. And I told them that was what I intended to do.

On Saturday, February 12, 2005, the members of the Democratic National Committee honored me by electing me to be the party chairman. In my acceptance speech, I told them what I had been telling them on the phone for weeks—that this wasn't going to be my chairmanship; it was going to be *our* chairmanship, and that I intended to listen to voices from outside the Beltway, the real voices of the Democratic Party.

I told them that we weren't going to cede a single voter or a single state. And I shared my belief that by standing up for our values, organizing, and transforming our party into a grassroots organization that can win in all fifty states, we would rebuild the Democratic Party, and victories at the polls would follow.

I took that message to the places where it needed to be heard. Immediately after I was elected chairman, I began what we called a "red, white, and blue" tour in several states that represented the breadth and diversity of America. In the space of seven days, I went to Kansas, New York, Michigan, Nevada, Oregon, and Mississippi. In each state, I talked to party leaders and met with activists. The visit that had the biggest impact on me, though, was Mississippi.

Mississippi is a state where Democrats have long since stopped competing for presidential electoral votes. We had lost races for the governorship and congressional seats as well. It's exactly the type of state too many Washington consultants have written off as red and unreachable. But when I got there, I saw something different. The eight-hundred-person ballroom was oversold, and hundreds of people waited in the hallways. There were so many, and they were so far from being able to see or hear what was going on, that we ordered dozens of pizzas just to give them something.

All four former Democratic governors were there. There was a palpable sense of new energy and new excitement. I told them that my election hadn't marked the end of the process of choosing a new chairman, but the beginning of the reemergence of the Democratic Party.

Surrounded by that energy, passion, and hope, I felt hope, too. These people, and millions like them in places that our party has too long neglected, are the faces of our future. Building on our existing strength, and finding new strength in new ideas and new supporters, I felt again that we did have the power to take back this country. I allowed myself to feel something I hadn't felt in a while: optimism.

The bottle of champagne that flight attendant gave me on Election Day is long since gone, given to a member of my staff. Democracy for America, by the way, continues to support fiscally conservative and socially progressive candidates. We're keeping the organization in the family, too. It will now be chaired by my brother, Jim, and run on a daily basis by Tom Hughes, who was the grassroots organizer for Dean for America in New Hampshire.

The hard work for me, and for all of us, is just beginning.

I think often of that room in Mississippi—that energy,

that hunger to win, and that willingness to get to work—
and I'm optimistic that Democrats will have a lot to cele-
brate in the days ahead.

Howard Dean
Burlington, Vermont
April 20, 2005

YOU HAVE THE POWER

★ 1 ★

From Anger to Hope

"I WANT MY COUNTRY BACK!"

The words just rose from my gut. And when they hit the room on that sunny March day in 2003, everything seemed to stop. The California Democrats, who only minutes earlier had been milling around, talking among themselves, and half listening as presidential candidate after candidate had made a play for their attention, paused. Everyone seemed to take a deep breath. And then the whole convention just exploded.

"WE WANT OUR COUNTRY BACK!"

"I don't want to be divided anymore," I said.

"I don't want to listen to the fundamentalist preachers anymore.

"I want America to look like America."

People were weeping quietly. Some were openly sobbing. Others were screaming. Standing on their chairs and stamping their feet.

Outside in the corridors, people were spontaneously writing checks and throwing them at my staff. They lined up, they mobbed us as we tried to make our way through the lobby. Some came away crying again, my aides later told me, *because they'd been able to touch my suit.*

My old $125 JCPenney suit.

I had no idea campaigning for president would mean becoming a part-time rock star. I was completely stunned. Overwhelmed. And humbled.

When I left the crowd and took off for the airport, when I got to the plane and found my seat, when the dust had settled and I was anonymous once again, I had a moment to reflect, and something became crystal clear:

What had happened in that room had very little to do with me. I'd been the catalyst for an eruption of feeling that was much deeper, more powerful, and, I would learn, more widespread than anything I'd ever imagined.

It was a low-burning fire of resentment and rage. All it needed was a simple spark in order to explode.

I ran for president because I was angry about where our country was going and I thought we could do better.

I was horrified by the way George W. Bush was governing our country. Mortgaging our future with irresponsible tax cuts for his friends. Despoiling our environment with huge giveaways to industry. Dividing us in the worst possible ways. Endangering our children with air pollution and draconian cuts in health-care services. Turning America into a monster in the eyes of the rest of the world.

I hadn't started out a Bush-basher. In fact, I'd been pre-disposed to like George Bush. I knew him personally and had dealt with him professionally when we were both governors. He'd always been charming and hospitable to me and my family, both in the Governor's Mansion in Texas and at the White House. He'd always been more than up-right in the business dealings between our states, keeping his word when he had no legal obligation to do so.[1] What I knew of his record in Texas bespoke a moderate man who was willing to put pragmatism before ideology, to raise taxes when necessary to equalize state education spending, and to take some heat from the right wing of his party for doing so. ("I hate those people," he'd once snarled at me when I ribbed him at a White House governors' gathering about some trouble he was having in Texas with the Christian Coalition.)

I'd approached his presidency with an open mind. I hadn't voted for Bush, but I didn't expect the worst of him, either. After all, I'd always been in the moderate middle of my own party—a staunch advocate of fiscal discipline, a devotee of balanced budgets, pro-choice but also pro–gun owners' rights, and in favor of the death penalty in some instances. In my races for governor, I'd always enjoyed the support of a certain number of moderate Republicans who shared my commitment to balanced budgets and responsible social spending. "Compassionate conservatism" sounded like something I could live with until the next Democrat ran. And from what I knew of George W. Bush's personality and temperament, I figured I could live with him, too.

I was astounded, then, when Bush cast moderation and conservatism aside and took up the mantle of right-wing extremism. He surrounded himself with radical ideologues and extremists: people who made a crusade of our foreign policy and polluted our government institutions with fundamentalist bigotry. I was shocked when the president set out to dismantle the social programs that Americans hold most dear: Social Security and Medicare. When he set out to undermine our system of public education with a bill called No Child Left Behind, which threatened to classify every public school in America as a failed institution within nine years. When he took aim at women through virulent anti-choice policies and at ethnic minorities through his repeated references to nonexistent "quotas."

None of this squared with the George Bush I knew. The lies and manipulations that lay behind such sham policies as No Child Left Behind (or No School Board Left Standing, as I came to call it) shocked me, coming from a man I remembered as having truly cared about things like education reform and improving opportunity for all children.

The sheer stupidity of much of what came out of the White House surprised me, because I knew firsthand that George W. Bush was not, by any means, a stupid man.

I doubted that he'd really changed his views. It seemed unlikely that he'd gone, in a matter of months, from moderation to the far side of the dark side of the American political spectrum. No—I concluded that once he'd gotten into the Oval Office, he'd become so disconnected from ordinary people and the details of their lives that he'd let the Republican Party's ideology get the better of him. He was missing the fine points of how that ideology affected ordinary people because he *just didn't care* about the details.

He painted the broad strokes of his policies and then left the details to Congress or the political hacks in his administration. Letting the chips fall where they might for millions of children. And sick people. And elderly Americans.

That lack of caring, that shrugging off of the details of ordinary Americans' lives, was every bit as enraging to me as purposeful, hateful extremism. It seemed to me, in some ways, even worse. It was callous and opportunistic. And it showed a willingness to put real people—real, ordinary Americans—in jeopardy.

Even more infuriating was the way my fellow Democrats went along for the ride, voting so much of the time to advance the president's perilous agenda. They approved his tax cuts, the Medicare prescription-drug act,

the war resolution, and educational "reforms"—all destructive measures that wouldn't have passed without
their support.

The Democrats were acting as though Bush had been
elected with a five-million-vote plurality and not, as was
the case, with five hundred thousand *fewer* popular votes
than Al Gore. They weren't acting like an opposition party.
They barely stood up to the president. When he asked for
his unaffordable and immoral $1.6 trillion in tax cuts, they
lay down and died.

One-point-six trillion? they protested. *Oh, no. Make it
$1.25 trillion. And not a penny more.*[2]

The Democrats were sweet-talked, they were bamboo-
zled, and they were afraid. They thought that by accommo-
dating the administration, they were somehow going to be
okay. In doing so, they helped the Republican Party pass its
far-right-wing agenda.

I thought: *Our people have to start acting like Democrats
again.*

I was far from alone in my thinking.

When I started feeling my way toward my campaign,
traveling around the country making appearances on behalf of other Democrats, talking about health care and
early childhood education, and then speaking out against
the war in Iraq, I came upon a lot of people who felt exactly
as I did. They were just like the people at the California
convention, bursting with resentment and desperate for
hope. They were profoundly angry both with President

Bush and with the Democrats who weren't doing anything to stand in his way. They were not only angry but scared and frustrated, because they saw their country changing in ways that threatened everything they cared about. And they felt powerless to stop it.

Their faith in our institutions had been eroded to a point where many of them hardly believed in the political process. In 1998 they'd seen their elected Congress suspend its responsibility to represent them and vote to impeach their president even though *two thirds of the electorate was against it.* In 2000 they'd seen right-wing appointees on the Supreme Court refuse to recount the Florida votes, overriding the rulings of the Florida Supreme Court, and essentially hand the presidency to their party's candidate.

They'd seen Republican protesters sent by Texas representative Tom DeLay, then the third most powerful Republican in the House, banging on windows and shaking their fists at vote counters in West Palm Beach, Florida;[3] African-American voters systematically turned away at the polls;[4] a family dynasty strong-arming election officials—overall, a political horror show worthy of a banana republic. It was the most serious attack on America's faith in democracy since the Tilden-Hayes debacle in 1876, when a Republican-dominated panel of congressmen, senators, and Supreme Court justices stepped in to decide a disputed election (with vote irregularities claimed in Florida, among other states). They ruled in favor of the Republican

candidate, Rutherford B. Hayes (earning Hayes the popular sobriquet of "Rutherfraud").[5] And it had sent a clear
message to the public: The Republicans had little respect
for our democratic institutions if they got in the way of
their party's agenda, and the Democrats were mostly
toothless when it came to fighting back.

The Republican assault on democracy didn't stop with
the election.

Next came a flurry of off-year congressional-district
gerrymandering, with a wink and a nod from the White
House, to give Republicans an advantage. House majority
leader Tom DeLay rammed a change through the Texas
House to redistrict in such a way that as many as five congressional Democratic seats could be lost with the stroke of
a pen. White House strategist Karl Rove personally lobbied
Colorado lawmakers by phone to get them to approve a re-
drawing of their state's congressional map to protect the
seat of a freshman Republican congressman who'd won
with only a 121-vote margin.[6] There were election irregularities in Alabama, where, after the polls were closed and
the press had gone home, six thousand votes were sud-
denly discovered that tipped the election away from the
Democratic governor to a Republican challenger. There
was the organized conservative effort to unseat an elected
governor in California. Then there was Supreme Court justice Anthony Scalia's duck-hunting junket with Vice President Dick Cheney, after which the justice refused to recuse

himself from the case Cheney had pending before the Court.

Even the plan adopted by Congress to deal with the Florida recount debacle—the Help America Vote Act— looked fixed from the start. No sooner had Congress authorized the states to buy new equipment to improve the reliability of future vote counting than the news came out that the new touch-screen voting machines were potentially *more* subject to tampering. Worse still, they left no paper trail. Worst of all: Two of the companies providing the new machines—Election Systems Software and Diebold Election Systems—had notable links to the Republican Party.[7] Most notably, Walden O'Dell, the CEO of the voting-machine maker Diebold Election Systems, had said in a fund-raising letter that he'd do all he could in "helping Ohio deliver its electoral votes for the President."[8]

The fix, it seemed, was in.

I spoke to African-Americans who said the Florida election debacle, with the reports of election-night police roadblocks in black neighborhoods, the wholesale removal of African-Americans from the voting rolls, and poll workers who turned black voters away brought back all too recent memories of the Jim Crow South. The whole experience had convinced them that the political system was hopelessly fixed against their interests. For a community already suspicious of our government institutions, this was a terrible blow—not just for them but for democracy. "People already didn't believe their votes counted," I heard. "Now they *know* they don't count."

This feeling of disenfranchisement wasn't limited to African-Americans or to the 2000 presidential vote. It came, more globally, from living in a society where ordinary people's problems and interests didn't seem to matter to their government. As the Bush administration passed measure after measure for the benefit of super-wealthy individuals and big corporations—the tax-cut bill, the Medicare prescription-drug act, and a whole slew of pro-industry environmental measures—it became increasingly clear that its true constituents were the people who paid for its campaigns.

And the Democrats—where were the Democrats?

Americans felt betrayed. Not only by their government but by their employers, many of whom were cutting benefits or downsizing or moving factories overseas. People who'd supported their families for decades were forced into shift work at places like Wal-Mart, earning minimum wage without health insurance, if they had jobs at all.

Americans were scared, too. Scared that there were more terror attacks to come, and that the administration's war on Iraq had made us more vulnerable. Many saw that they'd been lied to in the run-up to the war, and they were stunned by the extreme anti-American venom that had been unleashed because of those lies.

Americans were afraid that for all its military might, our country was on its way to becoming weaker. Weaker domestically, because people were demoralized and divided. Weaker internationally, because our moral authority was all but gone and because our foreign policy was being held hostage to an energy policy that made the procurement of large amounts of foreign oil a necessity.

People were angry, and they were cynical. They were depressed. They were caught off balance and confused—by the lies and manipulations of the Bush administration, and also by the fact that so many of the pillars of our society had proved in recent years to be so fragile. The Catholic Church scandals, the Florida recount, the Enron fiasco and other corporate corruption cases of its type: These were crises that went far beyond politics. They'd shaken up people's ability to believe in the essential rightness of our most basic institutions. Even the Monica Lewinsky scandal had broken a lot of people's hearts, because they'd seen not just their president but the presidency itself profoundly weakened.

People were aware of living in a world of anything-goes ethics. They were aware of being vulnerable to unpredictable catastrophic acts of terror. All of this made them doubt their leaders, doubt their future, doubt themselves. Young people—people too young to remember Watergate or Vietnam—were particularly hard hit psychologically, once the irrational confabulations that had led us into the war in Iraq were exposed. They'd grown up trusting in the basic good of the American government and the basic moral decency of its interventionist policies abroad. Now all this was crashing down around them, and they were at a loss to reassemble the pieces of their pride and their patriotism.[9]

This general crisis of confidence was something that no one—not Democrats, and certainly not Republicans—was finding words to address. Even the media, which sensed it, didn't get it.

I got it because, as an ordinary American living my life far outside the Beltway, I felt the way everyone else did. The only difference between me and most people was I had spent eleven years as a governor. I'd chaired the National Governors Association and the Democratic Governors' Association. So when I got mad, when I got sick of listening to myself complain, when I read *The New York Times* in my armchair and asked myself, *Well, are you going to sit there, or are you going to do something about it?* I was able to say, *Yes, I will. I will do something about it.*

I knew that I could, and in 2002, with my last term as governor drawing to a close, I was in a position to decide that I would.

So I opened a little campaign office in Montpelier. I began to travel around the country, governing on weekdays, meeting people on weekends, stumping for Democratic candidates, and getting out my message about health care and early childhood education and fiscal responsibility and the war.

As the governor of the second-smallest state in the country, I had no name recognition, to put it mildly, and no support from my party, to put it nicely. I had no campaign infrastructure, no press team, no handlers, no consultants, no "oppo research."

I would speak on behalf of candidates for other offices, share my views, tell the story of what I'd been able to do in Vermont, and then announce that I was running for president. People would go from looking interested to being amused. *You seem like a nice person*, their faces seemed to say, *and you've got some good ideas. But what makes you think an ordinary guy like you can run for president?*

I marched in a Greek Independence Day parade in Boston in the summer of 2002, and people shouted, "Governor!"—at Mike Dukakis. One man said he'd definitely vote for me—when I ran for mayor again.

Jim Jordan, John Kerry's former campaign manager, called me "an unemployed doctor with no responsibilities."[10] *The New York Times* mocked me for my lack of foreign-policy experience. *Everyone* went on about my so-called intemperate way of speaking ("mad-mouth disease," James Carville called it).[11]

But ordinary people didn't listen. Ordinary people started to think that having an ordinary guy run for president wasn't such a bad idea.

I realized in New York, and in Portland and Seattle—in all the places where I'd get up to speak and face a sea of people stretching back as far as I could see—that if you had something to say, people would come out to listen. I realized that people were *hungry* to listen if they came across a politician who really had something to say.

I realized, too, that people were thrilled to find a politician who reminded them of themselves. Someone who lived a normal life, with a wife and a family, who struggled to balance work and family, and sometimes got it right and sometimes didn't. Who shouted too loudly at hockey games and didn't always know the right thing to say. Who made "gaffes." Who disliked the media—and showed it. Who wore an old cheap suit and liked it, and traveled coach class and stood in line, and took the subway and ate too many doughnuts.

People felt they were like me. They felt they knew me. They followed my progress around the country on the blog entries that my campaign aide Kate O'Connor updated every day. If she wrote that we were eating too much junk food, people would show up at events with home-cooked meals. If I had a cold, they'd show up with cold medicines. They worried about me. If I misspoke, they scolded me. On the blog, they addressed me as "Guv."

They loved my wife, Judy, who kept up her medical practice while I toured the country. She chose to stay home to work and be with our seventeen-year-old son, Paul, a high school senior. To the media, this was poor campaign strategy. "Physician, heal thy spouse," wrote *The New York Times*'s Maureen Dowd.[12] But to regular people, it was great. They understood Judy because she was a normal person. Because, like them, she led a life filled with competing commitments and responsibilities. They understood her priorities—that you can't simply walk away from a job or a teenager at the drop of a hat, because children—and for her, patients—*need you to be around*. People got that.

Having a candidate who was like them clicked on a profound level with people. It suggested to them that they weren't alone. It made them feel listened to, as though they counted. And it made them feel, for the first time in a long time, that there was *hope* in a political landscape that, for as long as they could remember, had seemed all but closed to them and their concerns. To them, politicians seemed to care only about the interests of big-money donors. This flicker of hope, which the campaign ignited, soon turned into something more like a lightning bolt. It jolted people out of feeling disenfranchised and depressed. It made them feel empowered.

Jerome Groopman, a hematologist and oncologist at Harvard University, writes in his recent book, *The Anatomy of Hope*, that the ability to hope is the prerequisite for any patient's capacity to be cured. But people can't hope, he says, if they can't concretely see their way toward a cure.

And that's where a good doctor comes in: to devise and lay out a plan of action.

I know that he's right. As a physician, and as a local politician, I'd experienced many times, firsthand, what it looked and felt like to work with people and empower them to improve their lives after coming up with a plan of action to make it possible. I'd seen how hope, well-grounded hope, could have a transformational effect on people's lives. On the campaign trail, I was also seeing quite the opposite: Over the years, people had heard lots of nice-sounding words from politicians but gotten little in the way of reality-grounded hope. Instead of getting help with prescription-drug costs, they'd been given the Pharmaceutical Industry Give-Away Bill. Instead of getting help with education, they'd been given No Child Left Untested. Every four years candidates would come out and pretend to talk to them, but in reality, they were talking to the special interests who paid them. The voters pulled the levers on Election Day, but it was the special interests who really pulled the strings once Inauguration Day had passed.

Democratic voters in particular had gotten to the point, like patients who believe they're hopeless cases, where they'd practically lost their will to fight. They felt so disempowered, so *disenfranchised*, that they were almost unable to believe they were capable of taking control of their country's course. They were so worn down, so disillusioned, that they'd all but lost hope.

The fatal combination of Republican cravenness and Democratic cowardice wasn't having an awful effect solely on the U.S. economy. It was proving deeply scarring to the American psyche. Politics as usual was smothering the American will to believe.

Americans are a people unique in the world for their optimism, their faith, their ability to hope, and their belief that they can control their own fates. We are a relatively young country, uncynical by international standards, and though we've often been labeled by others as naive, our capacity for hope and faith and optimism has also made us a magnet for people seeking hope and faith and control over their lives from all over the globe.

It horrified me to see this strength of ours being squandered. It saddened me immeasurably to see the American spirit bending under the load of nonsense that passed for politics. It frightened me, too. I truly believe that much of America's power in the world comes from the fact that for so long, we've been able to inspire dreams of a better future in people around the world. Our source of power has been not our ability to bomb whole cities into oblivion, but our ability to peacefully captivate people's hearts and minds. It seemed to me that if we were failing to generate this power at home, then there was no way we could continue to do so overseas. The result was that we were seriously at risk of becoming a weak, second-rate nation.

• • •

In the beginning, my anger fueled the campaign. But then the tenor of my thinking changed. It happened sometime after that California speech to the Democrats, in the months surrounding my Sleepless Summer Tour, when I campaigned in eight states over four days. Somehow then, amid the fog of sleepless nights and crazy, multi-event-filled days, a series of images lodged in my mind.

A woman in a wheelchair in Iowa who handed me a bag of fifty dollars in quarters that she'd saved from her monthly disability check.

A young woman at Penn State University who'd read about the campaign on the Internet, then sent us a check for a hundred dollars with a note that said, "I sold my bicycle for Democracy."

A young man, Matt Gross, who drove from Utah to Vermont to set up our first Call to Action blog on the Internet. (I didn't even know what a blog was back then.) He didn't call first. He didn't check to see if he could have the job. He just showed up.

Manhattan's Bryant Park, filled to capacity. The Seattle square, set up for twelve hundred supporters, overflowing with ten thousand people spilling out into the surrounding streets, hanging out of windows . . . leaving me momentarily struck dumb with emotion.

It began to dawn on me that the people who came out to the rallies, who followed my campaign, often showing up at stop after stop in their state, weren't angry or depressed anymore. They were energized. Proud. Excited and happy.

They were full of hope.

I was feeling hopeful, too, as our numbers of declared supporters on the Internet swelled from an initial two thousand to more than seven hundred thousand, with millions more who didn't declare themselves online. As they raised a whopping $14.8 million in one quarter—a record for a Democratic candidate. As the number of people gathering to talk about the campaign through the Internet service Meetup swelled from about 400 to 190,000 in 180 cities nationwide.

At one point there were 850 Dean Meetup meetings a month! Thousands of people at a time were sending in donations of five and ten dollars over the Internet. One woman, Blanche Ramirez, who planned to get married in October 2003, decided to forgo a wedding registry and instead asked her guests to send contributions to my campaign. Another supporter's father died. She requested donations be sent to the campaign in lieu of flowers.

People were meeting up in all kinds of innovative, efficient, technologically unforeseeable ways that none of us—myself least of all—would have been clever enough to invent. Through DeanLink.com, Dean Wireless, and the GenDeanBlog. Through the Dean Yahoo! Groups, almost a

dozen in Oregon alone. People who had never been involved in politics organized voter registration drives and
fund-raisers. They wrote letters to strangers, sending more
than two hundred thousand handwritten letters to unde-
cided voters. They came up with some of our best campaign slogans. ("Give 'Em Health Care, Howard!" was a
popular one.) They ran Dean Corps volunteer projects to
make donations to food banks and clothing drives, to deliver toys to needy children during the holiday season, and
to volunteer in homeless shelters and in parks. They organized into Nurses for Dean. Seniors for Dean. African-
Americans for Dean. Latinos for Dean. And Alaskans for
Dean. The Dean DREAM (Diversify, Reach, Empower,
Activate, and Motivate) Team brought people together to
expand our grassroots organizing efforts in minority communities. The most remarkable thing about all of this was
that our supporters decided for the most part on their own
how they would help.

I knew I was witnessing something truly historic: the emer-
gence of a *real* grassroots political movement. It was the
start of something truly new. A campaign by, of, and for the
people.

Ordinary people, meeting up together, finding they
were no longer alone with their anger and fear and desire
for change, *felt empowered*. This changed their lives. They
started to see themselves differently. They found a new way
of looking at their lives and their relations to other people.

They found a new role for themselves in their towns and cities. In doing this, they found new communities, a new sense of connectedness, and greater empowerment within a larger community.

"This campaign has sparked a fire in me I have never seen," Blanche Ramirez, the bride-to-be, wrote to our blog. Howard Vicini, a leader of Seniors for Dean whose life had ground to a halt after decades of chronic pain and the total failure of our health-care system to care for him, wrote of finding himself "reacquainted . . . with hope and with the world-at-large . . . re-awakened to a spirit of community." Tracey Davey, a woman from Seattle who wrote to our blog about her battle with depression, said the campaign was "the best therapy anyone could ever hope for."

People felt as if they could do anything. First and foremost, as if they could take back America.

That, at base, was what my campaign was all about. It was not about me. It was not about my winning an election. It was about winning back America, from the ground up, and starting by remaking the election process. Putting people at the center. And making sure their voices were heard all the way back in Washington.

The people I met while campaigning for the presidency affected me every bit as much as I affected them.

Because of them, the reasons why I was running for president changed. The campaign wasn't just about replacing George Bush anymore. It was about bringing in a new vision for America. It wasn't about anger. It was about hope.

Which is why, when the campaign came to an end in February 2004, I knew that we—the American people—had won much more than I had lost by dropping out of the race. We had begun to change American electoral politics so much for the better, proving that it's possible—by circumventing corporate donors and going directly to the people—to raise tens of millions of dollars in five- and ten-dollar increments (or even in quarters). We'd proved that people could be roused from their sense of powerlessness and reinfused with hope. Just as long as there was someone to listen to them. To hear them. To respond to them honestly with words that had meaning. To empathize with their struggles. And to mirror their collective power.

I think now that of the many errors I made in the campaign, my most serious was failing to convey just how transformative getting to know America was for me. I stayed in attack mode long after it accurately reflected how I was feeling. It became a tactic. A persona. Which, in the hands of reporters (at whom I really *was* mad most of the time), gave me the public image of a guy who ate nails for breakfast. I never was that guy. But I thought—incorrectly, as it turns out—that in order to beat George Bush, I had to be. I wanted to make the point loud and clear: We weren't going to get the country back by having it *given* to us by the right wing. If we were going to get it back at all, we'd have to *take* it back.

You have to be tough to make it through a presidential campaign. You have to put your head down every day and keep on going. I'd learned this early on from Bill Bradley, who told me that I would set the tone of the campaign and I'd have to be as upbeat as I could be, especially with campaign staffers and supporters, because they would take their cue from me. So I remained upbeat. No matter what.

It was hard for me to lose the nomination. It was particularly hard because I felt so responsible for my supporters—those hundreds of thousands who'd invested themselves in the campaign. So many had quit their jobs and worked for seventeen hours a day on the campaign, with no money and no vacation. Many felt their lives had been changed by the campaign, so when it ended, abruptly, after riding so high for so long, they were left at loose ends. *You lifted us up and you dropped us down* was the message many of them wrote to me.

I knew how they felt. My life had been changed, too. Despite my continued efforts to stay cheerful in public and in front of my staff, I had plenty of dark moments of my own.

My campaign for president was built around the notion that we were going to bring all kinds of people in from all

around America and get the people in Washington to finally pay attention to them. The people from Washington
didn't like that idea very much. They didn't worry about it
much early on, when I was a nobody from nowhere. When
it looked as though we were going to win, however, it
scared the hell out of them. And they were willing to do
whatever it took to make sure we didn't win.

The attacks started in earnest after Al Gore endorsed
me. The Democrats began saying I was dangerously far
from the mainstream. The Democratic Leadership Council
sent out a memo calling my campaign "an aberration."[13]
Former Clinton strategist Dick Morris called me and my
ideas "permanent plagues on the Democratic Party."[14] Dick
Gephardt, in Iowa, repeated over and over again that I
was going to dismantle Social Security and Medicare. Joe
Lieberman let inferences be drawn that I was hostile to Israel.

I'd never gone through anything like that before. I'd
taken over a state after the governor had died in office,
which was a huge catastrophe, so I knew how to keep a
good face and move people forward. But I had never
endured the kinds of personal attacks that started once I
became the purported Democratic front-runner. It was
infuriating, for example, to go to New Hampshire and
see people at our rallies with Confederate flags, knowing
they'd been paid to do it by another Democratic campaign.

The worst moment of all came near the end of the
campaign. Before the Wisconsin primary, when things

were going badly, I learned that some of my Democratic rivals had created a secret political action committee to go after us in Iowa. They were spending $1 million to run negative ads attacking us. Robert Torricelli, the former Democratic senator from New Jersey who had to resign in a campaign-finance scandal, had personally sent fifty thousand dollars from his own campaign war chest for this effort.

This is the kind of tactic that Democrats and Republicans routinely use on each other in general elections. But I'd never seen Democrats doing it to one another, and I was furious. There was some comfort in thinking about how potent a threat my campaign must have seemed. But not much. The night I found out about the Torricelli donation, all I could think about was how low our party had sunk and how little I owed them.

It was by far the darkest moment I'd had—or was to have—on the campaign trail. This was a real crisis of faith. "Why am I doing this?" I wondered aloud. "Why am I a Democrat?"

I paced in my darkened hotel room in Milwaukee, making tracks in the carpet, my cell phone gripped tightly against my ear. "Why should I still be a Democrat after all this?"

On the other end of the line was Al Gore. Gore, who'd endorsed me at a time when it really mattered, who'd backed me every step of the way; who'd given me advice, tips on strategy, and incredible debriefings on the environment; Gore, who by reputation was a cold, cerebral man, basically talked me down off the ledge.

We hadn't known each other well before the campaign. Actually, we'd had some stormy times; me being me, I'd expressed my dissenting views on a policy question in 1992 with the less than diplomatic words: "You're wrong." Our relationship afterward was fairly stiff. But then I'd been blown away by a speech he gave about the war in Iraq in March 2003. I subsequently found out that Gore had written it himself. My admiration for him doubled again.

I started to call him for advice. Like every other Democratic candidate, I also called Bill Clinton for advice, and the contrast between the two of them was dramatic. While Clinton was an intuitive genius, Gore got to his thoughts by slowly and carefully putting things together, then testing his ideas again and again and again to make sure they were right.

Gore and I got to know each other over the phone, talking every month, then every few weeks, then spending time together on the campaign plane after his endorsement. Getting to know Al Gore turned out to be one of the most wonderful things that happened to me during the campaign. I realized that he was a lot of fun. A true friend. And even more obsessed than I was with the ins and outs of policy issues like global warming.

That night on the phone, he was extraordinary. Compassionate, not didactic—everything that his public image isn't. I hadn't yet won a primary. I knew Al wanted me to get out of the race (just like Tom Harkin and many of my other politically savvy supporters), and he knew I didn't want to go. After all, we had a good organization in Wisconsin. The people there had raised $1.5 million for us in small donations, and I'd promised them I was going to make my last stand in their state. I didn't want to quit. *We were so close.* We'd been leading in the polls until one week before the Iowa caucuses! I knew that if we won Iowa, we would win the whole thing, as John Kerry ultimately did. I wanted to try to at least come in second in Wisconsin. I felt I couldn't quit before trying.

So Gore didn't tell me to quit. He stayed up with me late that night and patiently, empathetically listened. When he spoke, he was right on target.

"Think long-term," he said. *"Keep your eye on where you really want to end up.*

"This isn't about whether or not Howard Dean ends up being president of the United States. It's about the future of the country."

No one else could have reached me then. No one else knew what it felt like to have things come crashing down around you when you were so close to winning. Only Al Gore could have known what it felt like to have been the leading candidate and be dethroned in the final hour. Al Gore had had the presidency in his grasp.

He was the one person in America who had the right to tell me whatever he damn well wanted. And only he could have been so right.

The Dean for America campaign was about much, much more than electing me to the White House. It was about reempowering people, and giving them hope, and providing them with the tools for rebuilding our democracy in their own image.

All of this, which we achieved to a surprising and unprecedented degree, didn't end when I dropped out of the race.

The hundreds of thousands of people who came into politics because of my campaign didn't disappear when it ended. They stayed and kept working. Many got involved in local elections. Some have run for office themselves.

In sum: Something happened in the course of our campaign that was very, very good for our country. People developed *hope*—and that, in and of itself, meant that they were more empowered.

They changed the process by which money was raised for an American presidential election. By making small donations that brought fund-raising to historic heights, they showed that it's possible to run for president without being beholden to special interests.

Through their participation, they did something Washington has never done—they enacted real campaign-finance reform. They brought ordinary people back to the center of a campaign on behalf of America. In so doing, they took the first, necessary step toward restoring democracy in America.

It's a necessary step, but not a sufficient one. Our campaign tapped into the transformational power of hope. Now, the Democratic Party has to move beyond the power of positive thinking. We need a clear, consistent, long-term commitment to a course of action that will give us a real hold on power in the years—and the decades—to come.

In this book, I'm going to talk about America as I found it on the campaign trail in the years leading up to the 2004 presidential election. I'm going to show how hope and faith and the power of the people were lost—and then found. And I'm going to propose a plan of action to ensure that ordinary people are never lost from the political process again. *You Have the Power* is a road map for the Democratic Party to follow so that it can become, once and for all, the party of ordinary Americans again. But it's not just for Democrats.

Ordinary Americans have to hold the Democrats' feet to the fire—so that real democracy can become an ingrained habit of mind.

We've got to open up the party's eyes and ears so that those in Washington will see past the anger they heard in my campaign to the suppressed hopes and dreams of the people who lifted their voices up in this election cycle.

We've got to make the Democratic Party the party of op-portunity and equality, of real American values, again. We can't just say it; we have to do it. We've got to distinguish ourselves by bringing out what's best in America: our spirit and our faith and our egalitarian impulse.

And we've got to be sure that ordinary people are never again forgotten by the political process. Because government "of the people, by the people and for the people" has no meaning if we let "the people" drop out of the equation.

★ 2 ★

Losing Our Country

Iowans are not, as a rule, a highly dramatic group of people.

So in 2002, when I met with a group of them in the back room of a small-town café, and I listened as they calmly and soberly described to me the precariousness of their lives, I knew that what I was hearing was not likely to be an exaggeration.

Yet the portrait they painted was stark: Their jobs—the lifeblood of their town—were all going to Mexico or China. With no good local jobs available to replace the ones lost, most people were planning to work at Wal-Mart. Part-time. With no benefits. If, they said, there were any part-time-no-benefit jobs left.

I'll never get the image of those sober-minded Iowans out of my mind, as they calmly explained to me about how their livelihoods were being shipped overseas. As I traveled to Michigan and Pennsylvania, to Wisconsin and Illinois and Oklahoma, stories like theirs rang continually in my ears. All across America, in small towns surrounded by farms, the one big local plant that employed the people trying to hold on to those farms was closing, and the multinational corporation that owned it was shipping jobs overseas. Leaving their former employees unemployed— and uninsured. They were being deprived of the most basic things they needed to feel safe and secure. And not just financially safe, psychologically safe as well.

The people I met couldn't get their minds around it: how, virtually from one day to the next, they could be sloughed off as if they had no history with their employers. Some of the people I met had been working in their local factory for twenty or thirty years. Some of their families had been in those factories for generations. They could remember what things had been like before, when employers had some loyalty. This new state of affairs—this world of big, faceless multinational corporations—it didn't feel like America to them anymore. And to have the government giving those companies tax breaks for shipping jobs overseas—well, that didn't feel like America, either.

People were seeing that there was no such thing as loyalty anymore in corporate America. Or, for that matter, in Washington.

They'd learned that they were expendable.

And that was a terrible lesson to take away from a lifetime of hard work.

· · ·

I heard many stories like this as I traveled across America during the campaign, getting to know people and the places they lived.

So many people lived with gnawing uncertainty about the future. So many seemed to be living close to the edge.

They had plenty of reasons to worry. Unemployment had reached a nine-year high of 6.4 percent.[1] Three point three million private-sector jobs had been lost,[2] and for the first time in seven years, workers' wages were growing more slowly than inflation. With wages stagnating, Americans were working longer hours and carrying more debt than at any time in our history. In 2003, a record 1.5 million people had filed for bankruptcy, and home foreclosures were at a record level.[3]

I met parents who worked two jobs to make ends meet, forced to choose between earning the money to provide for their children and spending the time to raise them.

I spoke with people who had worked for one company their entire lives, only to lose their pension because of the recklessness of their corporate bosses.

I spoke to families who'd sent their chief breadwinner off to the conflict in Iraq and now were barely scraping by. They were stunned when the Bush administration, despite its constant platitudes in support of the troops, tried to cut off the soldiers' hazardous-duty pay by declaring the Iraq conflict "over." The families wondered when the troops' ever lengthening tour of duty would end. They wondered if they'd be able to keep their homes. And they wondered where our government's loyalty was to its troops and to our veterans who were having their health-care benefits slashed while the president flew to Baghdad for a turkey dinner with the troops.

I met many, many people who had been pushed to the brink of bankruptcy because of unforeseen medical costs that were eating up their salaries and decimating their savings. So many Americans were losing their health insurance because they couldn't afford it anymore. Many were spending more on health care than for rent.

If these people were lucky, they came from supportive families or tight-knit communities. But it hardly mattered. Without a sure source of income, without a decent social safety net, they were often one step away from disaster.

Over and over, I heard the same questions: If our country is so rich, why am I barely getting by? If our country is so strong, why are we made to feel so afraid? If our country is so powerful, why do I feel so powerless?

People felt that in America, of all places, life shouldn't be so full of fear.

They felt that life in America was, in many ways, becoming unrecognizable.

Perhaps the biggest and most consistent misperception about our campaign was that it was a movement of young people. We did have a lot of young supporters, it's true: tens of thousands of active supporters under age thirty who brought incredible innovation and energy to the campaign.

But what our people had in common wasn't their youth.

What they had in common—what the vast majority of my most devoted supporters had in common—was the feeling of being disenfranchised.

There were baby boomers about my age, people who'd been deeply disillusioned by the trickery of Richard Nixon and had never really recovered. There were many others who had been devastated when the dreams of social justice bred in the 1960s started to fizzle out in the 1970s and 1980s and at the turn of the millennium.

There were people from minority communities who felt forgotten by the white majority and betrayed by the politicians they'd elected to speak up for them. They were thrilled to hear someone who was willing to speak out openly about inequality and race. There were moderate Republicans who felt betrayed by their party—disgusted by George Bush's big-spending profligacy and courting of the most extreme elements of the religious Right.

These were people of all stripes who had in common a feeling of having been neglected by the politicians they'd elected, ostensibly to serve and protect them. They were people who'd had it with politics as usual. And with being stressed. And with being afraid.

The situation I found on the campaign trail—this widespread sense of disenfranchisement—didn't happen overnight. It didn't originate with George W. Bush. It's the result of long-term political and economic decisions that have weakened the middle class, split Americans, torn apart our sense of community, and undermined our faith in our most important institutions.

America didn't always look the way it does today. It didn't always feel the way it does today. It looked and felt very different, for example, back when I was a child. Back when the "Greatest Generation" was settling down to raise their families. Back when Ronald Reagan was still a Democrat.

The United States emerged from World War II the most powerful country in the world. This wasn't just because it had won the war in Europe and the Far East and was enjoying a postwar economic boom that had created jobs at an incredible pace. It was also because the experience of the war had instilled an enormous feeling of solidarity among Americans. This solidarity played itself out, postwar, in government programs that together helped America build the largest and most powerful middle class in the world.

Programs like the GI Bill, which helped returning soldiers reinsert themselves into society and, through higher education and generous homeowner loans, propel their families upward into the middle class. Programs like Social Security, which began nationally in 1935, and Medicare, in 1965, which were founded to make sure Americans wouldn't end their lives in poverty or without medical care. Our public education system then was valued as a stabilizer of middle-class life and a vector into the middle class for immigrants and the poor. All this sent a message that America was one big community, and this bound people together.

Big companies, too, behaved like members of the community. When they did better, wages rose and benefits kept pace. They were offered incentives by the government to provide health and pension benefits to their workers. In all, the government and big corporations in the postwar period shared some of the risk with ordinary Americans, so if life threw you a curveball, you didn't have to deal with it entirely alone.

The net effect was that Americans were unified in the dream—and the emerging reality—of belonging to a comfortable, secure, and proud middle class. That created a sense of national community and shared responsibility that carried over, at its high point, into Lyndon Johnson's War on Poverty and the Civil Rights Act, which expanded the American community to embrace people formerly excluded by it. The Civil Rights Act and Johnson's antipoverty provisions expressed a true Democratic vision: that America was a country that would use its wealth and accumulated goodwill to better the lives of all of its citizens.

Unfortunately, this vision soon became clouded with ugliness. The rapid changes of the 1960s fed their own immediate backlash, which was exploited, with great success, by Richard Nixon. Nixon was the first president in my lifetime to willfully exploit issues such as race and income to divide Americans. He sought to cover up the inadequacies of Republican philosophy, which in Barry Goldwater's wake had come to be mainly about cutting taxes and consequently reducing the degree to which Americans were willing to be responsible for one another.

A philosophy that destroys community is a hard sell. So the Republicans, unable to offer much on issues like jobs, health care, and educational opportunities for all Americans, turned, from 1968 onward, to a strategy that aimed low rather than high. With nothing positive to say, they got Americans in the gut by playing to the fears and resentments that divided them.

Nixon encouraged the destruction of the American community with his so-called southern strategy, an attempt to pick up segregationist white southerners who'd previously supported Goldwater and George Wallace. He was unscrupulous in his divisiveness: He nominated two unqualified southern jurists for the Supreme Court, and when the Senate rejected them, he claimed anti-southern bias. He played the race card in every possible crass and crude way. It worked incredibly well, bringing him 86 percent of the white vote in the Deep South in 1968.[4] By turning his back on Johnson's civil rights legacy and appointing himself a spokesman for fearful, resentful, change-averse whites, he ensured the splitting up of America into two nations—black and white.

And yet however reactionary Nixon proved to be on race,

he was in other ways a true political moderate. He initiated the earned income tax credit, which relieved the tax burden of low-income working families. He created the Environmental Protection Agency. He proposed a plan for universal health care (which the Democrats turned down). He did not espouse the radical anti-government rhetoric of Barry Goldwater. That came later, with Ronald Reagan, who used his persuasive charm to bring the extreme Right into mainstream American politics. The effect of this was to split asunder not just blacks and whites but everyone outside of the upper reaches of the upper middle class.

On the campaign trail, this divisiveness played out in the new Republican obsession with hot-button social issues: the triad of "guns, God, and gays." But that was only window dressing. The bigger issue was that, under Reagan, a sizable income gap began to develop in America between the super-rich and everyone else, aided in large part by his tax policies, which lowered the tax rate on the top 1 percent of American families by almost 10 percent and raised payroll taxes, which fall disproportionately on working families.[5] These tax policies, combined with the enormous growth in wealth during the boom years of the 1980s and the tech bubble of the 1990s, led to the biggest redistribution of wealth seen in America since the time of Franklin D. Roosevelt. Except now, instead of wealth being spread more evenly to bolster the middle class and small businesses, it was being redistributed back up toward people at the top and to the world's largest corporations.

By the mid-1990s, the United States had been ranked by the United Nations as part of a "category of countries— among them Brazil, Britain and Guatemala—where the [wealth] gap is the worst around the world."[6] By 1998 the thirteen thousand richest families in America had incomes three hundred times that of average families, and almost as much income as the twenty million poorest households put together.[7] By 2000 there were 189 billionaires in America, with over $1 trillion in wealth. One percent of the population controlled 40 percent of the nation's wealth, while 20 percent of the nation's children were living in poverty.[8]

With mega-wealth came mega-power, as well as the increasing disempowerment of those without the means to buy the ear of their government. For Princeton economist Paul Krugman, this was a natural process: "As the gap between the rich and the rest of the population grows, economic policy increasingly caters to the interests of the elite, while public services for the population at large—above all, public education—are starved of resources," he wrote in *The New York Times Magazine* in 2002. "As policy increasingly favors the interests of the rich and neglects the interests of the general population, income disparities grow even wider."[9]

America had seen this before: in the robber-baron era at the turn of the last century, when a few ultra-wealthy captains of industry enjoyed a near total monopoly on much of the American marketplace and commanded an outsized degree of political power as well.

In this "new Gilded Age," as Krugman called it, a flood of special-interest money came into Washington and transformed the system of American government from one participated in by all to one accessible to a very few. With the wealth gap and corporate influence at unprecedented levels, we were living in what looked to many people like some kind of plutocracy.

This wasn't just the fault of the Republicans. It hadn't done much for people's faith in democracy to read about the kinds of donors the Democrats were cultivating for photo ops with the president and campaign contributions: from Chinese arms merchants to a convicted Colombian drug dealer to the Taiwanese businessman Johnny Chung, who, after having visited the White House at least forty-nine times, was later convicted of bank fraud, tax evasion, and conspiracy. It didn't send much of a message from the White House to Wall Street and the country at large about who was really in charge. Or perhaps it did: particularly in the Bush administration, when Harvey Pitt, a Wall Street lawyer who'd been outspoken in his distaste for government rules and regulations, was appointed chairman of the Securities and Exchange Commission (a job he used assiduously to avoid having to put into effect the reform legislation born of the 1990s corporate scandals).

In this period, ordinary people stopped running for

office. They didn't have the money to compete with the mega-millionaires and the operators backed by corporate millions who held the keys to the kingdom. In 1998 a record ninety seats went uncontested for the U.S. House of Representatives. "It is disconcerting to behold a political process that so matter-of-factly rewards unabashed competitive gluttony, a process so devoid of substantive discourse, a process so disdainful of the very people it is supposed to serve," the Center for Public Integrity's Charles Lewis wrote with disgust in 2000.[10]

There has always been a waxing and waning in the balance of power in America between ordinary people and the wealthy and well connected. Our founding fathers saw it coming and warned against letting the power of wealth outweigh the power of the ballot box. Teddy Roosevelt warned, too: "Every special interest is entitled to justice full, fair and complete . . . but not one is entitled to a vote in Congress, to a voice on the bench or to representation in any public office."[11]

In the past, times of excessive corporate ascendancy were followed by times of correction. FDR's New Deal so radically changed American society that it remained stable and protective of the middle class for half a century. But as the twenty-first century dawned and the Republicans grew more extreme and the Democrats grew more impotent, and our new Gilded Age ripened and began to grow rotten, no such correction seemed to be in sight.

The Democratic Party, just like the Republicans, emerged from the 1990s pretty much the captive of big-money interests. Some of its big donors were rich people who wanted to use their wealth to do the right thing for their country. But many, particularly the corporations, were *self-interested*. They hoped that when the time came, their interests would be recognized and they were pretty successful at seeing that happen. The Democrats in the 1990s supported telecom policies that failed to protect consumers and that accelerated the concentration of media power in corporate hands. While accepting generous corporate donations, they failed to build standards of corporate accountability or energetically go after corporate crime. Then under President Bush came an energy bill, written in secret by Vice President Dick Cheney and the oil industry. This was followed by the so-called Medicare prescription-drug act, which gave hundreds of billions of American taxpayer dollars to HMOs, drug companies, and the insurance industry and was so fiscally irresponsible that the administration was forced to conceal its true cost even from fellow Republicans in Congress.

Bush's tax cuts in 2001 and 2003 were an enormous giveaway to big corporations and the wealthy. Those tax cuts, dramatically reducing inheritance taxes and taxes on dividends, caused the wealthiest individuals' tax burden to fall from 28 percent in the 1990s to nearly 20 percent today. The corporate tax burden fell, too. In 1934 corporations had paid 30 to 40 percent of America's taxes, by 2003 they were paying about 13 percent. Cutting taxes while running up a huge debt load increasingly shifted wealth away from ordinary Americans, who were made responsible for paying off the government's debt. (By 2009, the share of national debt for a typical family of four will be $52,000.) The burden of maintaining a functioning society shifted to middle-class families, who were saddled with increased property taxes, health-insurance premiums, and college tuition. People who worked for a living paid more taxes; people who invested for a living paid fewer taxes.

The tax cuts almost entirely repudiated the notion that we might have a collective responsibility for one another. They widened the American wealth gap even further. They were a masterpiece of a radical agenda to destroy the social safety net and our public services through privatization and atrophy. They heralded a much lower standard of living for ordinary families while making corporations more profitable, thanks to tax subsidies. And they essentially shifted the burden of taxation from capital to hard work.

In response, ordinary people became demoralized. They stopped voting and checked out of politics, because they didn't think the political system was about them anymore. They didn't think their government was really there for them. To a large degree, they were right.

They were smart enough to know that the Bush administration's prescription-drug plan wasn't written for their benefit.

They could tell that the four-hundred-odd dollars they

got from the Bush tax cut was hush money to push through the tens of thousands of dollars gained each year by wealthy individuals.

They knew there was something rotten about a government in which oil companies were writing energy policy; in which big pharmaceutical companies were drafting Medicare reform without price competition; and in which a company formerly run by the vice president was awarded a $1.7 billion no-bid contract in a country where we were fighting an ill-conceived war.[12]

The increasing wealth gap—and the power gap that has come with it—has undermined American democracy. What the fracturing of America by wealth has led to is a general dismantling of Americans' sense of belonging to and having loyalty to a common, unified culture.

This has made it possible to sell people a bill of goods about dismantling social programs in order to improve their personal lot. That's the argument, for example, for school vouchers or tax cuts. These arguments fly because people are so used to being divided that they no longer think in terms of policies that could pull them together and make them collectively stronger. They don't see their common interests, so they don't vote with their common interests in mind. As Mickey Kaus put it in his 1992 book, *The End of Equality*, "Money is increasingly something that enables the rich, and even the merely prosperous, to live a life apart from the poor. And the rich and semi-rich increasingly seem to *want* to live a life apart . . . in part because they increasingly seem to feel that they deserve such a life. . . .[13]

By the time of the second Bush presidency, however, it wasn't just the poor who were so marginalized. It was the middle class as well.

Over the years, we've heard a great deal about the culture wars that divided the country after the 1960s: setting Left against Right, feminists against traditionalists, fundamentalists against secularists, members of minority groups against the white majority. The Republicans have manipulated these divisions again and again: Nixon with his southern strategy and Ronald Reagan with his "welfare queens," the first George Bush's presidential campaign with its Willie Horton ads and attacks on working women, and, most recently, George W. Bush with his scurrilous accusations about "quotas" in higher education and his completely gratuitous attempt to have the Constitution changed to formally restrict the rights of gays and lesbians.

While these battles raged—and were staged over time to generate media coverage—another insidious conflict has happened almost without comment. This other, more meaningful culture war has been fought between those seeking to increase and uphold the privileges of the wealthy and those seeking to save and defend the American middle class.

This culture war has pitted social Darwinism against social justice.

Or, it might be said, the free-dealing Texas subculture of George W. Bush and his cohorts against the Yankee communitarian culture that has molded my own ways of thinking and being.

In *American Dynasty*, his fascinating portrait of the Bush family and their world of influence, Kevin Phillips devotes a chapter to what he calls "Texanomics"—the combination of religion, fiscal policy, and local culture that, he writes, has made the state of Texas the place it is today. Which is to say: a place with one of the worst social welfare networks in the country. With one of the nation's highest percentages of uninsured children (two hundred thousand of whom would have been excluded from access to health care had Bush had his way as governor).[14]

In Texas, 40 percent of voters routinely vote Democratic. Texas has a strong progressive populist tradition. But you wouldn't know it by looking at the years since 1994, when George Bush became governor. It's now the state the Urban Institute has ranked worst of all fifty for its level of inequality among children. The state with the lowest level of per capita public spending (a matter of much local pride). The state responsible for some of the nation's worst environmental problems—not least because, as governor, Bush let industries write their own environmental regulations. In all, Phillips concludes, "Texas, as the 21st century opened, probably left more issues and circumstances unregulated—uncorrected, unameliorated, unassuaged—than any other state." It "had become the national capital of a politics that edged towards survival of the fittest." [15] Even *groundwater* in Texas, Phillips writes, is considered a private-property right.

The kind of social Darwinism you see in Texas and in the Bush administration—as well as in the culture of the Republican Party—holds that if you're rich you deserve it, and if you're poor you deserve it. Proponents of this view believe that the income gap ought to exist, because people ought to be rewarded more for the investment of their capital than for their labor; the fact that they have capital to invest means they've somehow proved themselves superior.

I can't subscribe to that. It goes against every fiber of my being, as the son of parents who took great pains to teach me that no matter how many privileges I enjoyed, I was never to think for a moment that I was better than anyone else.

My parents were a product of their time and their place. They belonged to a country club that "restricted" its membership, and they lived in a pretty rarefied world. But they didn't restrict their friendships to other people just like them. They taught my brothers and me that people had to be seen and understood as individuals—that you can't understand other people until you've walked a mile in their shoes. They also taught us a certain code of behavior: There was a way you were supposed to behave in life that had to do with treating people decently, even protectively. That code of behavior had a lot to do with why I initially thought I might be a teacher and later ended up in medicine. From teaching inner-city kids in New Haven and as a medical student in the South Bronx I learned that people have enormous, if sometimes hidden, potential and that we have to keep our eyes open to see that potential.

My father's life wasn't free of struggle. As a child, he battled diphtheria and came very close to losing: He had to have a tracheotomy tube from the time he was two until he was twelve. He lost his father when he was in his twenties. All this gave him, despite his otherwise privileged background, the capacity to walk a mile in the shoes of people who otherwise struggled. The same thing has been true for me.

When I graduated from college, I turned my back on much of what was expected of me—a certain kind of marriage, a certain kind of Wall Street career. I chose to make my own way, building a low-key life as a family doctor in a small rural state. This meant that I struggled for some years—not financially, but with the effort of going against the tide and forging my own identity. I had to carve out a place for myself in the world—like just about everyone else in America. This gave me, in the long run, a real ability to walk a mile in another man's shoes and to relate to other people, even if the cause of their struggles was far different from the causes of mine.

My politics are a direct reflection of the way I was raised and the place where I chose to make my life. Vermonters have a long cultural tradition of being responsible for one another. Not through handouts but through supporting people in ways that allow them to support themselves and be part of the larger community. Ours is a very nurturing state with a sense of neighborly obligation. You typically see this in rural states, where communities had to band together and take care of one another because they were relatively isolated and self-supporting. There's a strong ethic that says we're all in it together, and it translates into an almost ingrained sense of collective responsibility and a deep commitment to public programs that tie people together.

When I was governor, Vermont had a higher percentage of AmeriCorps volunteers than did any other state in the country. We had well-established social-welfare programs for the poor *and* the middle class. These programs began as low-income programs under my penultimate predecessor, Madeleine Kunin, and when I became governor, I expanded them to the middle class. We had universal health care for children whose families' incomes were up to $55,000 a year and child-care subsidies for families who made up to $40,000 a year. We ran parenting programs for poor families, hoping to help mothers and fathers who were overburdened and undersupported. The idea was to invest in people's potential so they could be the best parents and providers and members of our community that they could be. And we did it—by investing in those parents' potential, we brought some significant and permanent changes to the lives of Vermont's children.

We started offering the mothers of newborns in the state at-home visits from local social workers and nurses two weeks after their babies' births. Ninety percent accepted. Ten years later, child abuse rates for children under age six had dropped 43 percent. Sexual abuse rates for children under age six had dropped 70 percent. All because Vermonters believed that our community of like-minded, stable, middle-class citizens could be expanded to draw in people at risk. In other words, we really tried to help everyone enjoy the kind of security and stability that in much of America is now reserved for the upper reaches of the middle class and the wealthy. We rejected social Darwinism.

Vermont is a community built on compassion, frugality, hard work, and a sense of responsibility for other human beings. Our initiatives on behalf of children and families coexisted with fiscal conservatism. With a balanced budget. With a financial climate that was hospitable to business (much to the distress of my critics on the Left). This was because I knew that in order to fund the social-welfare programs I wanted to have in the state, we had to attract and hold on to local businesses—which we did. The banks and investment houses liked Vermont's fiscal situation so much that they raised our credit rating and reduced the cost of our borrowing.

We did what Republicans and Democrats in Washington have never been able to do: bring health care and child-care supports and good public schools and help with higher education to those outside the upper middle class—*without breaking the bank.*

We made our ideals about community and social responsibility into reality without getting caught up in overspending or spiraling debt.

Why, if we could do all this in Vermont, can't it be done in Washington?

As far as the Republicans are concerned, it's quite simple: They don't want to. The whole purpose of the Republican Party is to make sure corporate interests can do whatever they want to do, without people getting in the way. It's social Darwinism distilled down to its purest essence. And there's no room in it for collective responsibility or caring.

As for the Democrats, the party meant to protect working people and their families? In their case, it's a lot more complicated.

It has to do with internal party politics. And the corrupting power of corporate influence. And the inevitable calcification that set in toward the end of what I've come to call the forty-year reign.

★ 3 ★

Losing Our Party

Our lives begin to end the day we become silent about things that matter.

—MARTIN LUTHER KING, JR.

The last great moment of hope I recall in America was in 1992, when Bill Clinton was running for president. It was a similar moment, in many respects, to the one I witnessed on the campaign trail. A time of economic hardship, dislocation, and despair. A time when people felt particularly disconnected from their president, the first George Bush, who often showed them—most memorably when he failed to recognize a supermarket scanner—just how distant he was from the concerns of their daily lives.

Americans were fed up. They felt forgotten and taken for granted. So they turned to Bill Clinton, the man from

Hope, who gave the impression that he took no one for granted. They flocked to him. They *loved* him.

They mobbed him when he came up to campaign in Vermont and gave a big speech down on the waterfront.

"Help us believe again!" they shouted as Clinton and I rode together through the streets of Burlington after his speech. "You're our only hope!"

One woman came right up to the car window. She grabbed at his hand. "We need to hope again," she said. "Save us."

Bill Clinton was supposed to be a new kind of leader—an ordinary American who heard, and understood, the concerns of ordinary Americans. To a lot of people, desperate for deliverance after twelve years of Republican rule, he seemed like a savior. And for eight years, he did manage to stem the tide of the worst excesses of the Republican "revolution"—taking a stand against the often violent assault on women's reproductive rights; bringing a tone of inclusion and genuine compassion back to government; staking out a moral presence for America in other countries; and finally, ending the destructive downward spiral of deficit spending that had so rapidly accelerated under Ronald Reagan.

But the Democrats under Clinton didn't save the middle class.

In fact, despite his good intentions—and a genuine effort to create opportunities for middle- and working-class Americans that included raising the earned income tax credit and increasing the top marginal tax rate paid by the wealthiest Americans—the plight of the middle class worsened under Clinton's watch. Which may be why, in 2000, even with his admirable achievements, the country was so deeply, and for the Democrats, so fatally, divided between the two parties. After nearly a decade of widening income inequalities, campaign-finance scandals, noxious inside-the-Beltway compromises, and political catfights, people didn't feel there was much of a difference between the two parties.

The American people felt equally disenfranchised by Democrats and Republicans.

They weren't entirely wrong. While I do believe the Republicans are responsible for the lion's share of what has gone wrong in America over the past few decades, I don't think they are wholly to blame.

The Democratic Party has for some time failed to live up to its mission of being a party for ordinary people. While we haven't actively sought to undermine democracy and the American sense of community (as I believe the right-wing Republicans have done), we have neglected to *stop* the decline when we could have. We have sacrificed our core mission for what turned out to be erroneous short-term calculations about political viability. And we have lost the people's trust along the way.

I can still remember very well the day I got my first taste of national politics. It was August 12, 1980, the opening day of the Democratic National Convention in New York. I'd been sent to the convention as a Vermont delegate—a big step up from the envelope-licking I'd been doing on behalf of Jimmy Carter back home.

I was a big fan of Carter. I liked his politics, his honesty, and his decency. He was my kind of person—traditional, scientifically trained, an independent thinker. I liked the fact that he was an outsider and not too far to the left.

I'd never been comfortable with the hard-core Left. I was too distrustful of dogmatism. I didn't like the people who, if you didn't sign on for *their* kind of revolution, wrote you off as an irredeemable part of the bourgeois capitalist establishment. There were lots of those people around in the late 1960s and early 1970s, and for some of those years, they pretty much took over the Democratic Party. They pushed the party hard to the left, marginalizing the Democrats' traditional working-class and white ethnic supporters, many of whom tended to favor the war in Vietnam and to be relatively conservative on social issues. The party instituted quotas to make sure women and minorities were represented in its internal structure (which I approved of) and, in the name of inclusion, ushered in the era when identity politics would dominate the mainstream American Left.

All this was done, initially at least, with the best of intentions: to rid the party of the taint of segregation it had acquired during its history of supporting Jim Crow in the South. It was a noble thing to renounce racism and to take real steps to ensure that the party did more than merely talk the talk on civil rights. But these good intentions were corrupted in the late 1960s by the dark currents of hate, intolerance, and extremism that began to creep into the Far Left.

I'd come to the Democratic Party from Republican stock. As a teenager, I was a Goldwater Republican, just like my father (and, it should be noted, like then-teenage Hillary Rodham). Though my political views changed when I went to college and, like so many others of my generation, got caught up in the swing of the late 1960s, I never was a student radical or a firebrand. I broke with my parents' party, but I didn't practice politics as a form of adolescent rebellion. And while I was a progressive, firmly committed to the Democrats' values of equality and fairness, I was never tempted by the kind of ideological purism that led to infighting and the enforcement of political correctness.

As a political science major, I'd read enough Marx and Lenin, and knew enough about the suffering caused by communist ideology (in which the term "political correctness" originated), to disdain knee-jerk leftist rhetoric that romanticized socialism. I'd been horrified in 1970 when a group of anti-war protesters blew up a building at the University of Wisconsin–Madison that housed the Army Mathematics Research Center and killed a graduate student, Robert Fassnacht, just because he happened to be there at the wrong time. These actions, awful enough, were made worse by the group's sentiments afterward. "I'm sorry I didn't plan the bombing responsibly," Karleton Armstrong, one of the bombers, later said. "I don't feel bad about my motivations. . . . On the one hand, you feel bad. On the other hand, you feel pretty good."[1]

I thought this was inhuman. I thought then, as now, that extremism was a cancer, on the left just as on the right. I had no tolerance for intolerance in the service of a cause. My cause became centrism. Pragmatism. Inclusion. And principled compromise in service to the higher goal of getting good things done.

All of which, I thought, was the essence of Jimmy Carter's politics.

Attending the convention in New York was a life-changing experience for me. It was a real spectacle. The grand view. The sheer size of the thing—with different kinds of people from all over the country, every kind of American, and all different points of view (at least in the center Left)—was astounding.

It was nothing like the one other party convention I had attended: the 1964 Republican convention in San Francisco, where Nelson Rockefeller had been booed off the stage with people screaming and yelling insults at him. That event had had the atmosphere of a smoky white men's club. The Democratic convention was different. It was as diverse as America. But while there weren't any factions warring with the vituperation that the Goldwater Republicans had brought to the purge of Nelson Rockefeller, there were deep divisions on our side, too.

Our party still bore deep scars from the fighting that had torn it apart in the 1960s and early 1970s. In 1980 they were playing out in the primary battle between Senator Ted Kennedy and President Jimmy Carter. The differences between them were mostly about how to revive the country's failing economy: Carter wanted to do it through budget cuts, restricting government borrowing, and raising interest rates. Kennedy favored wage and price controls and a $12 billion jobs program. Carter wanted to reform welfare; Kennedy wanted to expand it. Carter thought that, rather than spending more, he ought to be doing whatever he could to balance the budget. This earned him the epithet of "Republican" from the supporters of Kennedy. But I thought he was on the right track.

When I came home from the convention, I became our party's local county chairman, chosen in part because Democrats felt I might somehow be able to bridge the gap and mediate between the two factions that, in 1980, were battling for the soul of the party: Carter's pragmatic, fiscally conservative centrists and Kennedy's younger, more liberal supporters. I was the same age as the young Kennedy reformers. But my history with the party, training with the pragmatic old-timers Esther Sorrell and Peg Hartigan, was all on the Carter side. This was where my heart lay, by temperament and belief. Still, I didn't dismiss the Kennedy people out of hand. And I didn't come across as a Carter diehard. Because I was accepted by both sides, I could see up close what worked and what didn't, and what was good for the party or wasn't.

Who could have guessed in 1980 that twenty-odd years later, self-avowed centrist Democrats would in fact be Republicans in all but name? And that I—a buttoned-down, unhip, boomer preppie, the most mainstream kind of mainstream American—would end up being tagged as a rabid left-wing radical?

Like so many other things that happened during my campaign, this ostensible metamorphosis had nothing to do with me and everything to do with the self-destruction of the Democratic Party.

The Democrats had the opportunity with Jimmy Carter to espouse long-term thinking. To see the value of reining in spending to balance the budget and continue to fund valued social programs into the future. To see the long-term usefulness of making change happen incrementally—gradually building programs like universal health coverage, for example, so they would have a chance to work without being economically infeasible and they could become an accepted part of the American social landscape.

Instead, we brought ourselves down. We poisoned ourselves by creating an ideological litmus test for candidates that pushed them out of the mainstream of American voters' beliefs and values. We let the perfect be the enemy of the good, and we made progress impossible through a kind of moral absolutism. This happened again and again in the Carter years—when activists from the Democratic Social-ist Organizing Committee picketed Congress over Carter's refusal to endorse the Humphrey-Hawkins Full Employ-ment Act, which would have required the government to make full employment a chief policy goal. It happened when senators refused the president's catastrophic health-insurance plan on the grounds that it wasn't comprehen-sive enough. It happened at the 1980 convention, when William Winpisinger, a Maryland delegate and president of the machinists' union, staged a walkout in protest of Carter's nomination. The Democrats scared people away from the party with talk of legalizing drugs, or of radical, crippling levels of income redistribution. We made it easy for Republicans to turn the term "liberal" into a dirty word and to paint the Democrats as out of touch for decades to come.

After Carter's defeat, the Democrats, out of favor and on the defensive, lost not only our hold on the presidency but our moral anchor. Although we kept control of Congress until 1994 (when it was wrenched away by a disgusted pub-lic), we failed *after forty years in power* to make good on our party's stated mission of sticking up for ordinary people. We *never* delivered on Harry Truman's call for universal health insurance. We failed to erect any kinds of safeguards to protect people against the economic trends and the Re-publican tax policies that gutted the middle class's sense of security. We dropped the ball on education. Labor rights. Child care. Even the environment.

After crippling ourselves through the rigidity of our (conflicting) principles, we stopped having any principles that anyone could discern at all, other than that of getting reelected. And when we were reelected, we worked our hardest to hold our turf and polish our images instead of getting the work of governing done.

I had a most unwelcome vision of this in 1991, when I first was governor and had been put in charge of health-care policy for the National Governors Association by Colorado governor Roy Romer, who had become my political mentor. Romer and I and a couple of other governors went down to Washington and met with the House leadership to discuss health-care reform. We had some ideas: We asked for changes in federal laws that were keeping states from working out their own plans for universal health coverage. The Democratic leadership refused to help us out. So I said, "Well, will *you* pass a health-care reform bill?" They said no. They said, "Too many people around here have been waiting their entire careers to pass this bill. We can't pass it right now; we don't have the votes. And *you're* not going to do it."

I quickly saw the big picture: These people had been waiting all their careers to pass health-care reform, but what they really cared about wasn't reform; it was their careers. And if waiting for "the right moment" for maximum career enhancement came at the expense of the 37 million

Americans who didn't have health insurance at that time, then so be it.

Many of the congressional Democrats wouldn't take a risk on anything that might be unpopular, be subject to attack, or allow other people to outshine them in getting some actual work done. So they wouldn't give a green light to the governors in 1991; and a few years later, they wouldn't hear the signals coming from Bob Dole that he was willing to compromise on Clinton's health-care plan. They were paralyzed between their fear of losing an election and their fear of change. In the end they lost and became the victims, in 1994, of the most sweeping congressional changes in sixty-two years. They set the table for Newt Gingrich. It was an awful irony: After decades of domination by the so-called party of the people, the party of FDR and Harry Truman, America continued, at the turn of the millennium, to be the only country in the industrialized world that didn't have health insurance for all its people.

The Democrats, who by the early 1990s had been in power in Congress without interruption for forty years, became so obsessed with keeping their seats and staving off challenges that they forgot why they were there. They lost sight of their mission to help the middle class maintain its standard of living and became obsessed with the maintenance of their own political careers. They turned their back on their core constituencies, in some cases under the guise of being "New Democrats." In fact, they relabeled their core constituencies "special-interest groups," whose influence, they tried to tell the public, had to be avoided like the plague.[2] ("A long-term majority," Democratic Leadership Council president Al From told *Time* magazine in 1995, "will never be created around the interests represented by Jesse [Jackson] and the labor unions.")[3]

The real problem, of course, is that Jesse Jackson and the labor unions form the core of the people who traditionally have elected Democrats. It is not an accident that members of labor unions and African-American voters became less interested in the Democratic Party as we crept to the right, and that we began to lose elections up and down the ballot with increasing regularity.

During my presidential campaign, I jokingly referred to the Democratic Leadership Council as the Republican wing of the Democratic Party. Some criticized this as a "gaffe." (The definition of a gaffe for Washington insiders is when you tell the truth and they think you shouldn't have.) Yet it is true that the DLC contributed, however inadvertently, to the ascendancy of the Republican Party by trumpeting the abandonment of the traditional values of the Democratic Party. We forgot that our values were what the people we represented needed, so our base became uninterested and despondent.

The Democrats, throughout the 1980s and early 1990s, didn't stick up for the people who were left behind by the Reagan revolution and the corporate restructuring that came at the end of the first Bush recession. Eschewing "class warfare," they didn't stick their necks out for the millions of Americans whose wages and living standards were frozen or falling. The Democrats missed the growing resentment of the "angry white men" who would later vote them out of Congress *because they just weren't listening*. And when the Democrats tried to catch up with the Republicans by belatedly wooing angry white men, they failed to understand that we needed to woo them differently—not with the unsubtle appeals to racism and homophobia used by the Republican Right, but with economic arguments. We began to soft-pedal our opposition to racism and downplay our remarkable achievements on civil rights under Lyndon Johnson. We became afraid of the Right, afraid of the anger, and instead of being steadfast, we pandered.

The Democratic Party has paid a big price for that. Worse, our people have paid a big price for the collapse of our will to lead. We failed to articulate a vision for America that keyed into Americans' hopes of overcoming economic and social instability. We lost the support of those looking for a positive way out. By remaining silent about all the things that mattered so much to Americans, we allowed ourselves to be painted into a corner and to be defined by the Republican opposition. By the early 1990s, we were known more for being the party of big government than for actually governing. And we were remembered, for as long as the Republicans could keep the stories alive, for a string of scandals reinforcing their assertions that we'd lost touch with good and decent American "values."

There were ridiculous things, epitomized by the time the chairman of the House Ways and Means Committee, Wilbur Mills (D-Arkansas), was caught in the company of stripper Fanne Foxe (his "Argentine firecracker"). Ms. Foxe chose to avoid the police by jumping out of Mills's Lincoln Continental and into the Tidal Basin. And there were not so ridiculous things like the sixty-nine charges of House rules violations that drove Democratic Speaker Jim Wright from office in 1989. Then came the string of rumors and other charges that roiled the House in a wave of scandal-scavenging that Wright, in his parting words, called "mindless cannibalism."[4]

In 1991 we saw the House banking and post office scandals. The bank scandal, which showed that members had been habitually overdrawn on their congressional bank accounts and were bouncing checks with impunity, implicated Democrats and Republicans alike, but the Republicans, campaigning against the Democratic-controlled Congress, were able to frame both scandals generally as the work of the "corrupt Democratic machine."[5]

There was some truth in that. The congressional Democrats, at the end of their forty-year reign, had begun to believe that the rules applying to every other American didn't apply to them. They were so secure in their power, and so effective at stifling dissent and keeping innovative young members down, that they were able to live within a bubble.

There was no challenge, there was no change. They awarded congressional chairmanships based on seniority, not on merit. Their take on governing was a mess of you-scratch-my-back-I'll-scratch-yours stuff, getting along and going along, and spending hundreds of millions of dollars on pork-barrel projects.

Ultimately, this laid the groundwork for the rise of the radical Right. It paved the way for clever hard-right-wing politicians with their ear to the ground and a cutting-edge grassroots infrastructure to captivate the attention of people frightened by the changes to America since the 1960s and disgusted by politics as usual. Newt Gingrich, in particular, spearheading the Republican drive for dominance in 1994, campaigned that year for reelection as though the entire Democratic-dominated 103rd Congress were his opponent, repeatedly blasting "gridlock," inefficiency, and the Democrats' imperial disdain for "normal Americans." Gingrich exploited the sense, shared by many Americans at the time, that the government took a whole lot more than it gave back to middle-class Americans. He maintained that there was no way the corrupt and decaying Congress could reform itself while Democrats remained in control.

This throw-the-bastards-out argument resonated so well with Americans that in the midterm elections of 1994, they handed the Republicans their first majority hold on both the House and the Senate since 1954, plus eleven new governorships.

At which point they got to work not on cleaning up and

reforming our democratic institutions but on trying to destroy them altogether.

They set their sights on eliminating eight entire government departments and agencies, and while they didn't pull it off (voters started to blanch when Republicans went after the Endangered Species Act and a host of other basic environmental, health and safety measures), they did manage to deal a near fatal blow to the Democrats. And not just to those in Congress. By establishing the Republican Congress—especially its Speaker—as a rival power source to the president, they sent shock waves right on up to the White House. The president of the United States felt compelled to state that he was "still relevant" after the election of the Republican Congress. This was like President Nixon's saying, "I am not a crook"—saying it raised the possibility that it was true.

There's no doubt that the lack of discipline in the Clinton White House in the first two years of his term—the lack of clear priorities, the insanely managed health-care-reform efforts, the gays-in-the-military controversy—played a big role in bringing Gingrich and his cohorts to power. Clinton knew this; he felt the weight of it terribly. It brought on one of those periodic episodes of self-flagellation that have punctuated the low points in his political life when he hangs his head, begs forgiveness, lets people criticize him, licks his wounds, and learns from his mistakes. It's part of his process of political recovery, and it has worked for him time and again. Not least of all because he's so very likable when he does it.

In 1981, after losing his first reelection campaign as governor, Clinton sought the counsel and forgiveness of passersby in his local supermarket. In 1995 he invited a group of Democratic governors to the White House.

It was a remarkable scene. There was the president, the most powerful man in the world, sitting at a table surrounded by six governors, inviting us to tell him why we thought he was in trouble and *taking it* when, with no holds barred, we did.

We took turns speaking, and when I told him I couldn't believe he'd allowed the gays-in-the-military controversy to outshine one of his major initiatives—the attempt to bring health care to all Americans—he bowed his head and covered his face with his hand.

I couldn't believe that a person so talented, intelligent, and committed could find himself in such a position. It felt like the beginning of the end.

But then I—like most people in 1995—was underestimating Bill Clinton, who managed not only to recover from 1994 but to win the presidential election of 1996 and to go on to oversee the most dramatic economic expansion in our nation's history. Many critics have said that he did so by essentially turning Republican himself, with welfare reform and the North American Free Trade Agreement being among the most stinging insults to the progressive forces that had once put their faith in him.

I think that criticism is unfair. Clinton had to balance the budget. He had to reform welfare—it was an institution obviously riddled with pathology that was not only harming the people it was meant to help but also increasingly turning Americans away from the idea of helping the poor altogether. His belief in the necessity of free-trade agreements was something that I supported until much later, when I first went to Iowa and saw what free trade had done to America's industrial heartland.

In retrospect, I see that it was incredibly shortsighted to believe that globalizing the advantages of world trade for multinational corporations, without globalizing protections for workers, human rights, and the environment, would lead to sustainable economic benefits for workers in the United States or anywhere else.

Free trade has brought stability to our relationship with countries such as China. It has forced the Chinese in particular, through economic integration with the rest of the world, to adhere more closely to international norms of constructive behavior. The real problem with free trade, however, is that the job is only half done, and unless we protect working people everywhere, open borders are ultimately unsustainable and probably incompatible with democracy.

It's fair to say that Clinton made too many compromises. On welfare reform, for example: Requiring mothers of young children to work long hours without providing them health insurance or child care was wrong. (In 1993, Vermont became the first state in America to enact a statewide welfare-reform project independent of the federal government, and we did it right: without time limits and with support for child care and health care.) But Clinton did what he could, given the limitations of working with an extreme-right-wing Congress.

But the booming economy that President Clinton oversaw covered up a lot of the damage to middle-class people that was going on underneath. The economy created its own sort of rosy haze, which meant that there wasn't any great pressure on the Clinton administration to do things like facilitate unionization in places like Wal-Mart, where many workers lack health insurance or a livable wage. There wasn't enormous pressure to get serious about how to preserve the middle class, because everyone was so caught up in the excitement of the dot-com phenomenon and the promise it seemed to hold of great riches for everyone.

Labor didn't push Clinton hard in the 1990s, because people were doing well overall, and unemployment was low. As for the jobs that were being lost overseas—well, everyone (including me) believed what Clinton believed, which was that the manufacturing-job losses that came as a result of the free-trade agreements would be made up with information-based jobs, for which workers could be educated and retrained. Clinton did put a lot of money into reeducation and retraining. But he wasn't prepared—none of us was—for the fact that when the dot-com bubble burst, knowledge-based jobs would go overseas, too, thanks to the Internet.

Bill Clinton deserves the full measure of credit for our country's amazing economic expansion in the 1990s. He was willing to take the tough steps (without a single Republican vote of support) to balance the budget. Without that kind of clear commitment on the part of the administration—a signal to investors around the world that America was worth investing in again—we never would have had the economic boom. For standing up for what was right for America, regardless of the political cost; for standing up for a balanced budget; for adhering to fiscal discipline when we needed it, Bill Clinton deserves accolades. Had Al Gore been elected, he would have inherited a projected $3.1 trillion[6] budget surplus, and with it an opportunity to restore hope to the American middle class. Instead, a new right-wing president shifted hard-earned middle-class tax dollars away from ordinary Americans to the corporate moguls who financed his ascension to the presidency.

Clinton tried to do the right thing on early childhood education and child-care policy. His administration scored modest victories in expanding health-care coverage for children. Furthermore, he had a substantive, pro-active, and morally concerned foreign policy. He kicked off the peace process in Northern Ireland. He nearly got an agreement signed between the Israelis and the Palestinians.

As far as I'm concerned, what's been problematic about Bill Clinton's presidency in the long term hasn't been the legacy of his policies. It's the way Democrats have drawn the wrong lesson from his success.

What the Democrats haven't understood is that the strategy they identify with him—of moving toward the center in order to compromise—worked for Clinton not because compromise was itself a successful strategy, but because *Bill Clinton was Bill Clinton*. A man with magnetism, charisma, and personal appeal on a scale that hasn't been seen in the Democratic Party since Franklin Roosevelt. A man with such boundless personal charm and political skills that he could walk out of virtually any room and leave the people in it convinced that he'd agreed with them without saying a single word to that effect. He was a man who could make big mistakes in the first two years of his presidency—with the poorly handled wrangle over the issue of gays in the military; the mess his administration made of their search for a female attorney general; the travel office "scandal"; and, of course, the health-care-reform fiasco—and survive. No other Democrat could have done it. Bill Clinton did only because he was so very exceptional. And because he knew how to come back, again and again, no matter how hard you hit him.

Bill Clinton hasn't succeeded, in life or as president, because he figured out how to work the system and make deals or move to the middle. He has succeeded because he is Bill Clinton. Which is why, even after Monica, even after he'd been impeached, his favorability ratings stood at a whopping 62 percent. Which is why, a little over a year ago, when I went to visit him up in his penthouse office in a social-services agency building in Harlem, people approached me as I walked up 125th Street and called out, "Hey, man, say hi to Brother Bill for me." (Everyone in Harlem knew where a group of white guys in suits was going on 125th Street.) Which is why the first printing of his 957-page political memoir was a mind-numbing 1.5 million copies.

Bill Clinton has a kind of personal magic. When he was running for president, and in the early years of his presidency, the mere idea of him made people feel empowered. The way he talked to them, the way he looked at them, the way he had of showing them that he was there for them and he was listening—all that was enough to make people feel good about themselves and feel as though they mattered. That's probably why so many people (outside of Washington) stood by him to the end. They kept him alive—partly because, after the impeachment, they were so appalled, perhaps even frightened, by the excesses of the right wing. They saw that plenty of Democrats had fallen into line with the Republican line of thinking on the Monica affair and that even those who voted against impeachment were loath to join with Hillary Clinton to lay the sordid exposure of the affair at the feet of a "vast right-wing conspiracy." Clinton—by simply struggling to maintain a shred of dignity in the face of an unbridled witch hunt—managed to convince people that he would fight back.

There's another problematic aspect of President Clinton's legacy. Bill Clinton was as impressed with big donors as they were with him. By cultivating them, he raised an enormous amount of money for the Democratic National Committee. But that didn't reinforce or expand the Democratic base in any way. In fact, the base contracted because ordinary people didn't feel valued by the party. With soft money at its height, in the years before the McCain-Feingold campaign-finance-reform bill passed, wealthy individuals were regularly writing huge, huge checks to the Democratic Party. This built the party's coffers, but it gave ordinary Americans the sense that they were irrelevant.

It was an enormous error, for a guy who has great vision, to fail to see the long-term consequences of allowing so many rich and powerful corporate types so much access to power in the Democratic Party, without a corresponding effort to see that average Americans also became invested. This oversight was ultimately the most serious blow to his political legacy. Early on, because of his own life story of rising from a modest background to Georgetown, Yale, and the White House, and thanks to his remarkable ability to connect with ordinary people, he made people feel empowered. But in the long term, because of the way he and other members of his administration cultivated wealthy and potentially generous donors, that sense of empowerment didn't last. Worse still: Bill Clinton set the stage for lesser mortals who did not possess his extraordinary charisma to think they could do the same and still keep the Democratic constituencies together.

Since he's been gone, the Democratic Leadership Council—the conservative policy group that Bill Clinton once chaired and used as a sounding board for many of the positions he ran on in the 1992 election—has been endlessly urging other Democrats to be like President Clinton. In rare moments of hubris, they even credited themselves for creating Clinton.

But they've consistently ignored the basic truth about Bill Clinton: He succeeded not because he was an accommodationist but because he had enormous political talent. He won not by moving to the middle but by giving hope to people and running against an administration that had little understanding of the lives of ordinary Americans. The problem with the "move to the middle" Clinton calculation, post-2001, has been that the middle has moved so far to the right that there aren't any real middle-of-the-road issues left anymore. The people running Congress are the kinds of people we used to snicker at when I was in high school—John Birchers, right-wing "wackos," as we called them.

The Democrats, by using appeasement as a political strategy, have solidified the Republican hold on power. Harry Truman once said, "When the voters are given the choice between voting for a Republican or a Democrat who acts like a Republican, they'll vote for the Republican every time." Our party made this come true in the 2002 midterm elections with dismaying results as, defying all expectations, the Republicans took control of the Senate, maintained their majority of governorships, and gained seats in the House. It was the first time in history that the Republicans had gained strength in the House in a midterm election while their party also held the White House.

In 2002, the Democrats misjudged the mood of the electorate. They thought they could get elected by playing it safe, moving to the middle, even by bragging that they'd voted with President Bush on most of his major legislative initiatives. Running on a record of having voted often with the Republicans cost Max Cleland and Jean Carnahan their respective seats in Georgia and Missouri. Abandoning his African-American running mate may well have helped to deny Governor Ronnie Musgrove his reelection in Mississippi. (Indeed, Democrats' chronic taking for granted of African-American voters threatens to cost us nationally in the years to come.) Whereas the party once enjoyed the near unanimous backing of the black population, fully 10 percent of African-Americans now vote Republican. Twenty-four percent now call themselves independents. And among the eighteen- to twenty-five-year-olds so important in future elections, that number is even higher.[7]

Democratic voters don't want to elect Republicans; they want Democrats with deep-seated principles. One Democratic observer quoted by *Washington Post* columnist E. J. Dionne, Jr., put it well: "They seem to believe more in their ideas than we do in ours."[8] In 2002, lacking anything worth voting for, Democratic voters didn't turn out. But the Republicans did, especially in Georgia—where, by using the issue of the flying of the Confederate flag, they unseated Roy Barnes, perhaps the nation's most effective governor, who had raised twenty times more money than his right-wing opponent.

The Democrats have made a fundamental mistake in watching Bill Clinton and thinking that it was his strategy—and not his extraordinary personality—that enabled him to do all the things he did. Instead of believing that reinventing some version of Bill Clinton can be our salvation, and grasping for a light that we can never reach, we should be getting back to winning elections the old-fashioned way: by listening and reaching out to voters. That, in fact, was the Bill Clinton way.

There are some who have argued, cynically, that there is no difference between the two major political parties in

America. That was the argument Ralph Nader made in both 2000 and 2004.

I'm not hostile to the idea of third-party candidates. Throughout America's history, third-party movements have often brought new ideas into our political culture. But what we have seen so far of the Bush presidency has shot holes in the argument that there is no difference between Democrats and Republicans.

George W. Bush ran in 2000 as a "compassionate conservative." His budgetary antics since then—with large cuts throughout our social-service networks, and the fastest-growing and largest deficits America has ever seen—have proved that he's neither compassionate nor conservative. He's a man who has despoiled our environment; sent our troops, under false pretenses, into a war that is unwinnable and unwise; and has divided us by race, sexual orientation, gender, religion, and income.

The Bush administration has attempted to increase the permissible amount of arsenic in our water, gutted the Clean Air Act, reversed the Clinton administration's roadless-area policy in national forests, and encouraged far more timbering at taxpayers' expense. His administration has attempted to drill in the Arctic National Wildlife Refuge and put people with gross conflicts of interest into key decision-making positions.

President Bush and today's Republican Party show no understanding of the connection between renewable energy and energy efficiency and our national defense. Our petrodollars end up partly funding organizations like Hamas and being funneled worldwide to fundamentalist Islamic schools that teach the hatred of Americans, Jews, moderate Muslims, and Christians.

To think that there is no difference between Democrats and Republicans on such key national security and environmental issues is not to think at all. And the differences continue, through issues like health care, education, the economy, and the future of the societal safety net that programs like Medicare and Social Security provide.

Democrats need to do a better job of making these distinctions clear and making our voices heard.

If we're going to win elections in the future, we have to live up to our purpose and our mission as the authentic party of the American people. We have to radically transform ourselves if we want to be able to reunite, reempower, and restore America.

This is a much bigger goal than winning one election cycle. At stake are the future strength and stability of our country.

We will not remain a powerful nation if we continue on the path of fiscal profligacy and inattention to the plight of the middle class that Republicans have set us on and sent us down. We can't project a strength abroad that we don't have at home.

Democrats must lead the charge to make America strong again. To do this, we must ourselves be strong.

We have to stand up for what we believe in. Say what we think and mean what we say. Most important, we have to be willing to say things that have meaning to ordinary Americans.

We need a real politics of meaning.

★ 4 ★

A *Real* Politics of Meaning

In April 1993, Hillary Clinton came in for many months of mockery when, during a speech to the University of Texas at Austin, she talked of the "alienation and despair and hopelessness" in America and called for a new "politics of meaning" to help restore the nation's spirit.

Afterward, the notion of this "politics of meaning" (a phrase borrowed from the philosopher Michael Lerner, editor of *Tikkun* magazine) got battered around on the left and on the right and was ridiculed as meaningless. Michael Kelly, mocking "Saint Hillary" in *The New York Times Magazine*, dismissed her views as the "gauzy and gushy wrappings of New Age jargon."[1] One columnist attacked her tone: "She sounded as if she's discovered spiritual truths that eluded Buddha and Jesus."[2] Others warned that her lofty words were just talk.[3]

The reaction to Hillary Clinton's speech was typical of what happens when the media gets a stick between its teeth and shakes and chews it down to the last splinter. It is also typical of how jaundiced people have become whenever anyone branches out beyond the banal rhetoric of everyday politics and tries to talk, as Hillary Clinton did, of larger values and beliefs.

For the past thirty-odd years, the language of values and belief and "meaning" in America in general has been monopolized by the radical Right. Right-wing ideologues have co-opted and corrupted so much of our language of inspiration—words like "patriotism" and "freedom" and "opportunity" and even "God"—that for many people, these words have become all but meaningless in the mouths of politicians. For Democrats in particular, these words have become suspect—"New Age jargon," in the opinion of much of the media, sheer manipulation to the ears of much of our public.

This has left a terrible void, both in the heart of our party and in the soul of the nation.

For years Democrats have been afraid to talk about faith or values. We've avoided taking a moral tone or speaking too strongly about patriotic pride. This has played right into the hands of the Republicans, who long ago keyed into something that we are still too nervous to face: Americans are a deeply religious people.[4] A deeply patriotic people. An idealistic and optimistic people who yearn, deep in their hearts, to hear and feel things like Reagan's "It's morning in America."

For decades, with the exception of Bill Clinton in 1992,

the Republicans have beat us at every turn in the battle for Americans' hearts and minds. They have been more successful in reading the national mood, more attuned to the wishes and desires (and fears) of their grass roots, and generally better able to talk the talk that Americans want to hear.

This didn't happen accidentally. The "Republican noise machine,"[5] as former conservative mudslinger David Brock has called it, didn't gear up overnight. The Republicans trained for it. Their party took pains to educate its troops in verbal warfare. They worked with pollsters like the conservative pundit Frank Luntz, who instructed their candidates in the proper use and misuse of political vocabulary. For example: A 1990 mailing sent by Newt Gingrich to the "farm team" of up-and-coming Republican candidates contained specific instructions on using words to best advantage against the Democrats. Called "Language, a Key Mechanism of Control," it included a list of 133 words divided into two sections: "Optimistic Positive Governing Words" (i.e., "your message") and "Contrasting Words," to be used to "help you define the policies and record of your opponent and the Democratic Party." The good words included liberty, commitment, opportunity, pride, duty, truth, reform, choice, we/us/our dream, and freedom. The bad words included welfare, hypocrisy, corrupt, radical, status quo, permissive attitude, unionized, ideological, intolerant, and red tape.[6]

But the Republicans didn't only choose their words with care; over the years, they perfected the art of twisting them subtly (and not so subtly) to keep their meaning in line with their politics.

"Family values" became code for a right-wing crusade against working women and gays and lesbians. Talk of "community" meant communities turned against one another. "Personal responsibility" provided cover for irresponsible government practices that stiffed the poor. "Faith" was put to the service of religious bigotry. All of this lofty rhetoric that seemed to play to our best impulses was used to cloak the Republicans' mean-spiritedness and appeal to Americans' worst natures.

The Republicans, maneuvering brilliantly under the guidance of their language czars, learned how to cloak their radical ideology—an ideology far more extreme than what most Americans accept—in words that sounded mainstream. *Contract with America*, the 1994 campaign document that announced the battle plan of Gingrich's Republican revolution, was conceived by Luntz, who'd worked as a pollster for both Pat Buchanan and Ross Perot in 1992, to appeal to moderate Republican voters by hiding the hard-right wing's social agenda. After Gingrich became Speaker, Brock reports in *The Republican Noise Machine*, Luntz tutored newly elected Republicans in Congress on how to sell their radical agenda to more socially progressive neocons through careful turns of phrase. For example:

The estate tax was to be called a "death tax" and school vouchers thereafter to be known as "opportunity scholarships."[7]

The result of all this has been an American disaster: the mainstreaming of an anti-democratic, anti-pluralistic, openly theocratic agenda. The biggest coup of all: bringing a team of radical-right-wing ideologues to the White House under cover of "compassionate conservatism." Democrats— and moderate Republicans—now have woken up and found ourselves in an America ruled by people pushing forward intolerant, discriminatory policies—anti-woman, anti-gay, anti–civil liberties—all in the name of God. The truth is, we allowed this to happen by remaining mostly silent about the things that give meaning to people's lives.

The theft of meaning—of truth and faith and the ability to believe—has been one of the worst things the Republicans have done to the American people. It's time for the Democrats to fight back. We've got to fight fire with fire. Not by cynically co-opting the language of religion for our own purposes, or by blurring the line between church and state, or by aping the self-righteousness of the right wing. But by challenging their charade of virtue with a *real* politics of meaning.

I am a Christian, and it seems to me that the right wing of the Republican Party preaches virtue on the one hand and intolerance on the other, while welcoming the money changers into the temple of government. Jesus spent most of his days ministering to lepers, prostitutes, and Samaritans and advocating care for the poor. Those who wave the Bible as a threat to sinners ought to open it once in a while to learn from the teachings of Christ. Democrats can easily make the argument that our traditional mission of standing up for the disenfranchised follows the teachings of Jesus much more closely than do the modern-day Pharisees of the Right.

How do we create a real politics of meaning? First, by opposing and exposing the Republicans' smoke-and-mirrors style of communication. Then, by showing America a genuinely inclusive vision for our future. This requires a political program based on saying what we mean, doing what we say and *bringing real change* to the American public. We've got to bring people change not just at the level of political rhetoric, or even in the intricacies of political policies, but right at the level of what our policies mean—which values they reflect and which deeper truths they reveal about the nature of American society. Our policies need to be transparent, allowing us to see the values that went into creating them.

Democrats are uniquely well positioned to strive for this. Unlike the Republicans, we have nothing to hide. Our basic values—of equality, fairness, opportunity for all, pluralism *and* freedom, and religious faith coexisting with the separation of church and state—are the same basic values shared by the vast majority of Americans. They are also the basis for American democracy.

The opportunity is fully ours now to show Americans how we can put those values into practice at home and abroad. If we can do this, we will not only emerge, once and for all, as the majority party in America. We will also restore Americans' faith in themselves and in democracy. Here's how:

We need to model real moral leadership.

It used to be that when the eyes of the outside world fell upon America, what they saw was a beacon of hope, opportunity, and openness, of freedom and human decency. This vision remained largely unchanged from the founding of our nation until the end of the last millennium (despite serious opposition in much of the world to our actions in Vietnam).

In the last three years, the moral leadership of America in the world has been lost. This administration's actions before and during the Iraq war—the falsifications; the international bullying; the humiliations visited upon foreign leaders who opposed us, such as Gerhard Schröder of Germany and Vicente Fox of Mexico; the flouting of the Geneva Conventions; the Abu Ghraib prison scandal and revelations of other abuses in prisons in Afghanistan and Guantánamo Bay—have made us seem like a very different kind of nation to the outside world. Most Americans can't recognize their country in the pictures of shackled and hooded Iraqis undergoing psychological and sometimes physical torture. The sense of shame at home and the hatred of us abroad that this president's vindictive foreign-policy style has spawned is not consistent with the way we Americans see ourselves, or with our humanitarian values.

There is an enormous amount of repair work to do. We need to continue the efforts started by Bill Clinton to use to positive ends our standing as the world's only superpower. It isn't enough for us to be the most powerful nation in the world militarily. We need to be a moral leader, proving our strength by projecting abroad our values, our beliefs, and the best aspects of our way of life. We need a foreign policy designed to inspire rather than intimidate. We need a defense policy that will secure our people's long-term safety by blunting our enemies' abilities to create foot soldiers of hate.

I supported President Bush's retaliatory war on the Taliban and his father's 1991 war to free Kuwait from Iraqi rule. When there is just cause or a clear and present danger, I fully believe that America must use military force, and I think our armed forces must be kept up to the task. I also supported Bill Clinton's interventions in Bosnia and Kosovo when the Europeans shamefully failed to act to stem the slaughter of Bosnian Muslims and later Kosovars. One of the roles of the last remaining superpower is to be part policeman, like it or not.

But the real battleground of the twenty-first century is in the hearts and minds of the millions of people around the globe who are increasingly being persuaded to turn against us. Whether it's because they've fallen under the sway of an anti-Western ideology that demands our demise, or because they despise our friendship with Israel, or because the trickle-down effects of globalization have pooled in such a way that nothing but envy and resentment are making their way down to them, the decentralized army of people hostile to America is growing. And they can't be stopped by conventional military strategies. They can't be located by GPS monitors or obliterated by smart bombs, and certainly not by tactical battlefield nuclear weapons.

We can't fight them as we fought the Soviet Union during the Cold War, by attacking their ideology head on and building up weapons of mass destruction. Doing so is not only self-destructive (as is the Iraq war, waged with the remnants of Cold War thinking passed down by the Cheneys and Rumsfelds of this administration), it is pointless. A militarily strong America—isolated and alienated from the rest of the world, creating chaos and danger, inspiring hatred and fear—will be tomorrow's former superpower.

We need to project our strengths abroad, not our fears and weaknesses. We need to export, along with the products and business practices that have flooded the globe these past ten years, our energy, our generosity, and our openness of spirit. We need to export a love of freedom, democracy, and independent thinking. Again, not by imposing it militarily but by modeling it through our behavior with other nations in matters of security and trade.

This isn't to say that we should never stand up publicly

and confront our allies—as well as our enemies—for the sake of what's right. We justly criticized the Europeans for doing nothing to stop the Southeastern European conflagration until we acted first. We should criticize the Saudis, who smile at us with one side of their mouth while, with the other, they permit their citizens to fund the teaching of hate throughout the globe.

But our foreign policy should never rely on humiliation. Humiliation is a weapon that can leave scars far deeper than those inflicted by armed conflict. The deliberate public snubbing of Prime Minister Schröder, President Fox, and earlier, President Kim Dae Jung of South Korea changed fundamental attitudes about America held by Germans, Mexicans, and South Koreans, and not for the better. To be the moral leader of the world, we need a strong military and a strong spine. But we also need to extend a hand to others who wish to deal with us in good faith. We need to work with the United Nations and to rebuild our long-term alliances. We need to conduct our foreign policy with respect and humility. It won't be taken as a sign of weakness. It will signal our confidence and strength.

Americans can't dictate to other nations the course that their cultures can take. But we can tilt the playing field to reward societies that are trying to modernize and move away from practices that are incompatible with the values of the modern world, such as slavery, murderous tribalism and nationalism, and the suppression of equal rights for women. Harry Truman did an enormous amount to enable the Europeans to build what has become the European Union through the Marshall Plan, allowing the broken nations on both sides of World War II to begin economic recovery. Fifty years later, the EU has significantly reduced the kind of European nationalism that had spawned a thousand years of war on the most troubled continent on earth. A new American policy that creates modern-day Marshall Plans in Africa, the Middle East, and Latin America ought to be the goal of a new American president.

The marketplace can hand out rewards, and our commercial presence within other nations can be a powerful source of positive change and inspiration, *if we conduct ourselves in a positively inspiring way.*

Fifteen years into the era of globalization, we still have a long way to go to be consistently inspiring. The truth is, the fruits of globalization have not been distributed in anything vaguely resembling a fair and egalitarian way. The United States is not entirely to blame for this. But as the leading champion of globalization—and the chief proponent of the view that exporting the American way of doing business will lead to the spread of a free, egalitarian, and prosperous way of life—we bear a significant responsibility for making sure that the promises of our economic expansion overseas don't seem disingenuous to ordinary working people in other nations.

For the sake of our nation's own safety and for the purpose of practicing what we preach abroad, Democrats have to step forward now and complete the revolution in world trade practices that began under Bill Clinton. We must provide, once more, moral leadership in pushing for new trade agreements that protect the environment and guarantee the rights and living standards of workers at home and around the globe.

We have to make sure that globalization isn't just a boon for multinational corporations (and, all too often, corrupt governments that starve their people while feeding off of those corporations). We have to make sure that our global commercial practices really do advance the cause of freedom and democracy, rather than adding to the disenfranchisement of people around the world.

For too long, Democrats have been depicted as weak on defense, somehow lacking in patriotism, and unable to project America's glory and strength abroad. This is nonsense, and we can prove it. Simply by acting on our values, by *standing up and being Democrats again,* we can restore America's standing in the world community. We can make Americans feel secure, because our foreign and domestic policies will keep America safer. We can make Americans feel proud, because our foreign and domestic policies will inspire the world's respect. We can restore the American dream, because we will rekindle faith and hope in America at home and in other nations.

We need to rebuild the American middle class.

The Republicans' support of tax cuts, of "small government" and deregulation, isn't simply an economic position.

It's a moral and ethical (in my mind, unethical) position. It's a philosophical worldview that seeps into every aspect of their politics and values.

Ever since the time of Ronald Reagan, Republicans have spread the message in this country and abroad that the way to wealth and national health is through a kind of rugged individualism that means never acknowledging our interdependence as human beings. This was presented as somehow integral to our national character—even though our nation was built by communities in rural areas and uncharted outposts facing the challenges of life together. It has, of course, been in the interest of Republicans to stress self-reliance and individualism. That's the Frank Luntz way of packaging their economic plans to starve support for the needy.

But leaving people on their own to flounder and drown doesn't really reflect the values of most Americans. The policies based on this philosophy of social Darwinism haven't made America strong; they've made middle-class America weaker by draining resources away from families. By taking our own money away from civic life and community activism. By encouraging selfishness. By making people *feel alone.*

As I argued earlier, America didn't become the dominant world leader of the late twentieth century by being a nation of citizens "bowling alone" (as the title of Harvard public-policy professor Robert Putnam's 2000 book on the breakdown of American community put it), but rather by strengthening and building up its middle class. Democratic support for labor unions and programs like the GI Bill helped create a coherent and unified sense of national community where, if you were willing to work hard and serve your country, you could count on being able to afford a middle-class lifestyle.

Those were Democratic achievements. Rebuilding the American community and moving it forward into the twenty-first century will be a Democratic accomplishment as well. To do that, we must once again put our basic principles and values into practice, through policies explicitly conceived to restore national unity. Economically, the way to do that is by building up the middle class again and rejecting the notion that the way to win elections is to become Republicans lite. The only "special interest" that ought to matter to our government should be the American people. Until we learn that, we won't be winning many elections.

We've got to do nationally what we did in Vermont: build a social safety net, not just for poor people but for the middle class, so that hardworking parents can go to sleep at night without worrying about being able to obtain decent child care or about their kids not having health insurance or about not having enough money to pay for college.

We've got to bring middle-class American families universal health insurance, child-care subsidies, and student-loan programs that work. We also must change our current tax laws to promote progressive tax policies. We need a fair and simple tax code—a moral tax code—in which hard work is rewarded, wealth pays its fair share, and corporations pay what they truly owe, more if they pollute or otherwise fail to live up to the standards of our national community. Our current federal system of taxation is regressive, in that it disproportionately affects people of modest incomes. Middle-class people pay a higher percentage of their disposable income in taxes than do wealthy investors. Warren Buffett, the billionaire investor with a conscience, once wrote an article decrying the fact that one of his secretaries who made thirty thousand dollars a year was in a higher tax bracket than he was. That is the case because our political leaders don't care about secretaries, but they do care about billionaires: Billionaires finance campaigns. We can have an America that is better than this.

The Social Security tax takes the largest bite out of many wage-earners' paychecks. But because it is capped at an annual income level of $87,000, a school superintendent who makes, say, $87,000 a year pays the same payroll tax as a CEO who makes $40 million a year. This is not only unjust, it's guaranteeing the collapse of our Social Security system, an event that the right wing has long sought. The fix is easy: Eliminate the cap and make payroll taxes less regressive. Then people who make $50,000 a year won't be in a higher tax bracket than people who make $500,000 a year.

Under the Republicans, work has been taxed more and more while wealth is taxed less. Many companies that leave a mess of pollution for us to clean up, or are sending jobs overseas, have been subsidized by the taxes their own employees pay to the federal treasury. All of this is wrong. And it's not consistent with the values of our national community. We have to shift the burden of tax payment to achieve a fair balance for everyone who benefits from what this country offers.

We also have to ensure that people can earn a living wage, because an individual can't even begin to live on the $5.15 that our government now considers an acceptable minimum wage. Giving people a decent living wage is a basic act of social justice that extends the possibility of empowerment to those who need it the most. While I don't think—as some advocates for a living wage do—that it's feasible or plausible to expect businesses to pay the $10.87 an hour most workers need to live properly, I do think that the Democrats should make it a priority to raise the minimum wage to $7 (as we did in Vermont) and make up as much of the remaining $3.87 as possible through programs like food stamps, universal health care, middle-class childcare subsidies, and heating subsidies—supports that help people maintain the building blocks of life in our society.

We also have to make sure all Americans have access to good public schools. The public school system in America has served us extraordinarily well, making it possible for people to come to this country with nothing and to work their way up, over the course of a generation or two, to participate fully in the American dream. The public school system gives a note of universality to the American experience that is of enormous importance to us as a national community.

We can't afford to starve and undermine our public schools, as the Republicans have been doing with the so-called No Child Left Behind. We can't afford to marginalize and impoverish the public school experience, which is where the movement to create federally funded private school vouchers will lead. The public school system is the first and last place in America where everybody has to get along with everybody else, no matter what their ethnic or religious or racial or neighborhood background. It is the building block of the American community, the great socializing experience for future citizens able to instinctively understand what community means. Instead of attacking public education, we ought to give parents more and better choices within the public school system.

Democrats can't change our society in any meaningful and lasting way if we don't support the public schools. We can't have a different kind of government—a government that provides for and protects its people—if people haven't learned how to recognize their common interests.

That's why I also believe we ought to back—and greatly expand—programs like AmeriCorps. We need some form of national service for young people that allows them to give back to America and develop a sense of connectedness to their country. During the campaign, I proposed an expansion of this great program that could draw young people together from all walks of life and from all over the country for two years after high school. It would offer them the chance to do public service projects—cleaning up streams, looking in on isolated seniors, tutoring kids in failing schools—in exchange for help with college tuition. Most important, it would give them a chance to work with and learn to understand people very different from themselves. We had a program like this in Vermont that I started, a public-private partnership called the Youth Conservation Corps. It was a huge success, particularly because, unlike AmeriCorps (which generally draws middle-class kids), it brought together middle-class and lower-income kids.

Also in the campaign, I proposed what I believe to be a workable student-loan program in which every student enrolled in college or a post–high school technical school would be eligible for a ten-thousand-dollar-a-year government loan for four years; after graduation, they would pay back the loan using no more than 10 percent of their income each year for ten years. (People who went into public service professions—like nursing or police work or fire-fighting or teaching—would pay just 7.5 percent of their income each year for ten years.) An expanded AmeriCorps and a student-loan program of this type would cost only about $7 billion *a year.* This is a drop in the ocean of our government's $2.1 trillion annual budget, and a bargain when you consider the $300 billion annual price tag of the Bush tax cuts. It's not a lot of money when you consider the payoff. But it's an impossible sum to find when public moneys are being spent instead on filling the coffers of big corporations. Just one example: Shortly before this book's printing, Congress was asked to spend $5 billion to fix a corporate tax subsidy that had been declared illegal by the World Trade Organization. The House, under the leadership of Tom DeLay and Speaker Dennis Hastert, passed a bill that cost the taxpayers $167 billion: $5 billion to fix the subsidy problem and $162 billion worth of pork for Congress to send to their favorite causes. That pork would buy a lot of education and health care for America's middle class.

We should not waste money on policies—like the Bush tax cuts—that destroy America as a community.

We need to replace policies that weaken us with policies that will build back our strength.

We need to replace the politics of division with a politics of unity.

George W. Bush, a "Spanish-speaking" president from a border state, came into office with the potential to bring the voices of America's ethnic minorities right to the heart of Washington. But his immigration policies, his window-dressing appointments of African-Americans and Latinos (Bill Clinton's government, by contrast, really did look like America, up and down the line), and his repeated use of the racist code word "quotas" regarding affirmative action have proved that he's just another Republican happy to conquer by dividing.

Republicans have used divisive language to exploit racial and ethnic tensions since the days of Richard Nixon.

But the Democrats, too—while officially the party of minorities—have for decades employed a way of talking about race that divides people rather than uniting them. You see it in the "identity politics" of the Left, which are based upon a notion that what race or ethnicity or gender you are determines how you think, what you want, and who you are. This form of politics reached its nadir in the early 1990s, contributing to the backlash voiced by hyper-conservatives like Rush Limbaugh. It continues in the way political campaigns are conducted today: with members of minority groups assigned to special "outreach" desks, narrowly devising tactics or events that cater to what's perceived to be the special demands of particular "interest groups." ("No wonder they hate us," a high-level campaign staffer recently groused to me as she contemplated the tiny, marginalized pod of outreach desks in the headquarters of a Democratic campaign operation.)

I think this way of talking to—and about—people in minority communities is wrong. Democrats must start talking about race in a way that says there's much more uniting us than dividing us.

During the campaign, I was once asked at a fund-raiser in Washington, D.C., "What are you going to do for the African-American community?"

I didn't have to give the question a moment's thought. "I'll do just what I said I'd do for all communities in America," I answered. Afterward, the man who asked me the question—who was himself African-American—came up to me and said, "That's exactly the right answer. I'm so glad you didn't fall into the trap of telling me all the things that you're going to do just for black people."

The Democrats need to face the fact that all people, deep down, want the same things. Everybody needs a job, white, black, Latino, man, woman, gay, or straight. Everyone heeds health insurance, American Indian, Asian-American, Muslim, Jew, or Christian. Every American needs good schools and a chance to go to college. There are issues of special importance for each of us: immigration reform, affirmative action, abortion rights, civil rights, and sovereignty issues. But 95 percent of what we are interested in is shared. That is to say: We care about the same things—issues that touch us, and our loved ones, in our daily lives.

This was one of the lessons I learned in Burlington in the 1980s, when I worked in the state legislature during the day and came home to practice medicine at night. I quickly saw that the people I was treating didn't give a damn about the $1 million I had fought over in the legislature for some social program. What they wanted to know about was their back pain, and what they wanted to tell me about was their marriage problems or their job stresses or the worries they had about their kids. Those are the concerns people live with every day. What they want from their government, and from politicians, is for us to understand the basics. What Democrats need to know is that the basics are for everyone.

The Democrats have their hearts in the right place on race issues, but they haven't figured out how to talk about them yet. We need a new way of talking about race. And not just to minorities but to white people. Particularly to those white people who don't normally talk or think about race. The way to do it is not by preaching to them or making them feel guilty. It's by gently dealing with the human frailties—such as racism, conscious or not—that each of us possesses.

There's a story I often like to tell when I talk to crowds about race. It tells how, when I was governor of Vermont, I always had a woman as my chief of staff. My chief of staff did the hiring. And my office was essentially a matriarchy. The vast majority of all the senior staff positions were filled by women; about half the cabinet were women. As it turned out, half of the judges I appointed were women, too; in fact, during my tenure, we had the highest percentage of senior women executives of any state government in America.

One day my then chief of staff came to my office and told me she was going to hire a new policy analyst because we'd lost somebody who had moved into a job outside of the government. "I just want you to know you'll probably see a new face around here," she said.

Normally, I would have thanked her for telling me and moved on to other business. But this time I said, "Let's discuss this for a moment. There's a tremendous gender imbalance in this office, and I wonder if you could find a *man* for this position."

She looked at me and immediately answered, "You know, Governor, you're right. There really is a gender imbalance in the office. But it's so hard to find a qualified *man*."

This story always makes people laugh. And it makes them think—and possibly it makes them call their behavior into question and maybe even change it.

When I tell this story in racially mixed audiences, I sometimes add another story told to me by an African-American Washingtonian who is a political consultant. He told me how he helped a young African-American get elected to the city council in Washington for the first time. The consultant was put in charge of hiring the new council member's staff. When the staff gathered for the first time, they sat around the table, looked one another over, and said, "Uh-oh." Everybody in that room was male and African-American.

All people can recognize themselves in stories like this. It's not just fifty-five-year-old white men like me who think, consciously or not, that hiring people just like themselves is better than hiring people who are different. Women do it. African-Americans do it. Everybody does it, and it doesn't mean that you're a racist or a bigot if you do. It just means that every human being has an innate tendency to be ethnocentric, and to hire or socialize in an ethnocentric way. But in a country as diverse as ours, with one group of people, white men, doing most of the hiring, ethnocentrism hurts America.

Telling stories like this, using personal experience and getting people to relate to one another by showing them their similarities, is the most effective way I know for getting people to think and talk productively about race. Because that's how people's attitudes change—not in broad sweeping strokes based on principle, but by becoming able to walk a mile in the shoes of someone they once found irreconcilably different. Overcoming an ingrained sense of difference is the precondition to recognizing and attacking racism from the ground up. It is also a prerequisite for getting Americans to see the 95 percent we have in common and not be so focused on the 5 percent that makes us different.

I saw this up close in Vermont when I dealt with the issue of gay marriage.

In 1999 our state supreme court ruled that our marriage laws were unconstitutional because they were discriminatory. Married people had certain rights—inheritance rights, tax privileges, literally thousands of rights— that unmarried or single people didn't. The court ruled this not just unfair but unconstitutional, because there are a significant number of people who are not allowed to get married simply because they're gay or lesbian. Unlike the supreme court in Massachusetts, which basically told legislators what they had to do, our court then gave our legislature the task of designing a remedy.

When this happened, I said I was uncomfortable with the idea of gay marriage. I was immediately criticized, but I thought it was worthwhile to be honest. After all, like many Americans, I had lived almost all my life in a culture that was pretty anti-gay. Like a lot of other Americans, I'd snickered at the locker-room jokes, listened to my parents and teachers and ministers, and picked up a lot of things about gay people that weren't nice or true. However, having grown up during the civil rights movement, I also believed that equal rights under the law could not be abridged no matter what I thought about gay marriage. I was determined to get a bill passed that guaranteed equal rights under the law, at least in Vermont, which was the limit of my jurisdiction.

I was invited to many, many gay groups and got to know a lot of gay, lesbian, bisexual, and transgendered Americans well. I realized that there wasn't anything different about gay people, except that they fell in love with people of the same sex. It was just what I had learned about Jews or Muslims or Latinos or evangelical Christians or anyone else: There wasn't anything fundamentally different between us in terms of what our needs were, what our cares were, what our strengths were, and what our weaknesses were as human beings.

People kept coming up to me during the legislative session, saying, "Can we study this until after the next election?" I said no, we had to pass some kind of bill. What we came up with was a compromise: a civil union bill that gave equal rights to every couple. We created a parallel institution to marriage, with a different name, because marriage was entwined with many people's religious beliefs. Our compromise gave gay and lesbian couples in our state all the same rights that heterosexual couples had except those rights accorded by the federal government, which were outside of our purview. And that needs to be fixed as well.

For me, in the end, the civil-union issue was a straightforward question of getting people equal rights under the law. But it led to a painful debate in our state, with much more bitterness than we've seen in Massachusetts. Once the House had voted for the civil unions bill and we were getting closer to enacting it, there was an outpouring of anger and ugliness from all over the country. We had established, respectable churches coming to Vermont to tell us that we were all going to hell. Especially me.

Which, of course, remains to be seen.

It remains to be seen, too, just how much my support for the civil unions bill will hurt my chances to reshape Democratic politics.

Whatever the cost of signing the civil unions bill, it was worth it. It was my first experience of doing something that, with the stroke of a pen, directly empowered a whole group of Americans. After I signed the bill, a lot of people from Vermont's gay and lesbian community wanted to talk to me about it. When they did, I began to realize, up close, just what it had meant to them. It was an act of validation.

A recognition of their identity. Something truly life-changing for a group of people who had so often in the past had to hide who they were.

I also saw the incredibly positive effect that dealing with this issue had on other people. How thinking it through—listening, for example, to mothers and fathers who came to the state Capitol to tell us what it was like to have a child who was forever discriminated against or excluded—affected people right down to their very core. Well-meaning straight people who didn't initially support the bill because they didn't understand the need for it were swayed when they came to understand, in a way they never had before, what life is like if you're gay and unprotected by law in America. There was a remarkable woman—Marion Milne, a Republican—who was so appalled by the outpouring of hate the civil unions bill generated that she ended up supporting it, precisely because all that hate made her stop and say to herself: *If this is what gay people have to put up with, then I have no choice but to stand up for them.* There were legislators who voted for the bill knowing that it could be the end of their political careers. In fact, a lot of wonderful people who voted for the bill, including Marion, did lose their seats in the legislature as a result.

We all, in a sense, may have been consigned to hell by the forces of the status quo, hostile to difference and change. But which is worse: becoming "unviable" or remaining silent on things that matter?

It is impossible to love America and hate Americans of

any kind. Prejudice, bigotry, racism—these aren't the kinds of problems that will fix themselves or fade away under the weight of good intentions. But they can be fixed if people can be made to see their common humanity. If each American can be led to figure out his or her personal biases and watch out for them. Because we all have them, every single one of us. And overcoming them is something we have to work on every day, every single moment, when you interact with other people.

Our party, working above all at a grassroots level, can bring about this change. We can make different kinds of people come together in common cause all over the nation. Just as it happened during my campaign. And in Vermont over the issue of civil unions.

The way many well-meaning heterosexuals originally viewed the gay-rights situation is the same way well-meaning white people often don't think their views are hurtful to their black neighbors. Many white people think racism isn't a problem anymore. They're wrong, of course: In 2003, *The Wall Street Journal* wrote a story about a study that showed that white job applicants with drug convictions were more likely to be called back for a second job interview than were equally qualified black applicants who had clean records. White people often don't see racism as it operates around them. That's not because they're bigoted or even particularly ignorant. It's because they don't have the eyes to see it, by virtue of being white.

I remember how shocked I was to hear my African-

American roommates and friends in college tell stories about being followed around in stores. One of my roommates told me that when he came to visit me in New York, he was asked if he'd like to go up in the service elevator. This was a real eye-opener for me. So was the experience of being in our suite some evenings when we were sitting around talking and playing music and looking around and realizing that everyone in the room was black except for me. For a moment I'd think: *What if it were always like this for me? What if I were the only white person and everyone I knew was black?* It gave me a tiny insight into what it was like to be a member of a minority community. Yet it was only a hypothetical. It would have been a very different situation if life had stayed the way it was in that room forever.

I had requested to live with African-American roommates when I started college. I'd just come back from a year abroad on an exchange scholarship, where one of my closest friends was Muslim, from northern Nigeria. I thought it was time I learned something about an America I knew nothing about: black America.

You could argue that my openness to other people, my acceptance of difference and the changes in the late 1960s that were making Yale—and my world in general—a much more diverse place, were actually a privilege that came along with my upbringing. I was sure of my place in society and never afraid that opening up my world to new people would mean that I'd be somehow diminished or have fewer opportunities. I was coming of age at a time when jobs were plentiful. And I was, thanks to my father, sheltered from much of the insecurity of the outside world. I never feared that assuring a place at the table for other people threatened my own.

It's often different for people who struggle to make ends meet. It's easy for them to fall prey to politicians who'll take advantage of their struggles to blame, for example, women or minorities for their problems. This is what Nixon did when he made the play for the Wallace and Goldwater vote with his southern strategy. It's what Jesse Helms did in 1990, when, in a race against a black opponent, he ran a campaign ad that showed a white man crumpling up a rejection letter as a voice-over said, "You needed that job, and you were the best qualified. But they had to give it to a minority because of a racial quota. Is that really fair?"[8] This kind of manipulation, of scapegoating, of using code words and racism to win elections, has gone on for decades—in the same period, not coincidentally, when the gross income inequalities that really divided people were allowed and encouraged to flourish. It's time Democrats stepped forward to stop it.

We need to appeal to what's best in America.

The Republicans have for decades consistently appealed to the worst in us. We have to do the opposite. And the way we can do it is by articulating a *real politics of inclusion*. Not just pretty words about our "melting pot" or "salad bowl," but policies that draw everyone together in recognition of our common interests: adequate health care, an excellent education, the assurance that they can have a decent job at a living wage, and the confidence that they'll be secure in their retirement and able to maintain a reasonable quality of life in their senior years.

This is what I tried to express with such controversial results during my campaign in my much repeated comment about "people who drive pickup trucks with Confederate flags." The full context of that line, as I first delivered it in a speech to the Democratic National Convention in February 2003, was this: "I intend to talk about race during this election in the South. The Republicans have been talking about it since 1968 in order to divide us, and I'm going to bring us together. Because you know what? White folks in the South who drive pickup trucks with Confederate flag decals on the back ought to be voting with us, because their kids don't have health insurance, either, and their kids need better schools."

People who heard me say this then, and in subsequent speeches, got exactly what I meant—and African-Americans seemed to get it the most. They knew from unfortunate past experience that it isn't by segregating and stigmatizing people that we will create real community in America. It's by talking to them as members of one community—as Americans—and leading them to discover their common interests and humanity.

We are not yet far enough away from the Faustian bargain made in the South between right-wing politicians and working-class whites, which was: We won't raise you up, but as long as you don't complain, we'll make sure there's someone down below you. This is the essence of the pitch made to struggling white southerners by the Republican Party. What I was trying to say in the campaign to working-class whites was this: *There's no need for anybody to be down.* We can all have health insurance for our kids; we can all have decent schools, just as long as we see that keeping people down doesn't do any of us—outside of the right wing of the Republican Party—any good.

Don Payne, vice-chairman of the Congressional Black Caucus from New Jersey, once said to me that southern white working people were the most underrepresented people in America. If you're black in the South, he said, you can get some help from the Congressional Black Caucus. But if you're white and working-class in the South and you vote for these right-wing politicians who forget about you as soon as they cross the state line for D.C., you have no one to be your advocate. Your kids never do get health care, and they never do get decent schools, and they never do get opportunities to move up, because the real allegiance of the people you've voted for is to the corporations and big-business people who financed their campaigns—not to you.

I think he's absolutely right. If enough people can be shown that he's right, then we'll see some real change in

America. If people can come to see their common interests, they'll have enormous collective power to demand the things from Washington that really make a difference in their lives.

The way to bring people to this isn't by getting in their face or making them feel evil. It's by talking about our prejudices by using examples that have resonance in their personal lives. By showing people the price that both whites and blacks pay for racism. By teaching white politicians to talk about race in front of white audiences. To get white politicians to lead on racial issues the way Lyndon Johnson, Harry Truman, and Robert Kennedy did. By getting white politicians from northern states to understand that racism in the North is not only as prevalent as it is in the South, it is more insidious. Look at school systems in Milwaukee or Chicago or Newark, New Jersey. They are as segregated as any in the South. Most of all, we need to appeal to the best in people and allow them to set aside the things that cause pain and hate—which are mostly fear and misunderstanding.

I tried to do this on the campaign trail. The Democrats have to do it now. But they can't do it only in stump speeches or in the hallowed halls of Washington. We need an army of people who are willing to go out and talk about their personal experiences, a grassroots movement to rebuild American community, much like the one I discovered during my campaign. And it has started. In 2004, Democracy ForAmerica.com, founded in the wake of my presidential campaign, endorsed eight hundred candidates running for mostly local offices around the country. One of these was a twenty-eight-year-old social worker with no previous elective experience, an African-American woman named Maria Chappelle-Nadal who is running for the Missouri House of Representatives from the St. Louis area. The district is about 50 percent African-American and 50 percent white; her opponents are two more-established African-American politicians. On a campaign trip for her, I saw droves of young white progressives not only supporting her (a phenomenon that began during Jesse Jackson's 1984 presidential campaign) but working for her, organizing for her, in paid positions alongside African-American staff. It used to be that white progressives and African-American organizers formed an uneasy alliance. This one seemed easy and natural. The younger generation has come so much further than mine in a much shorter time, and in this case, they came through. Maria Chapelle-Nadal won her race and is now serving in the Missouri House of Representatives.

I think that most Americans share my hope for a unified national community. The values of equality and the rejection of bigotry are now deeply ingrained in mainstream America. The Republicans know this—that's why you get so much lip service about equal opportunity coming from the otherwise opportunity-crushing right wing. That's why George Bush got elected on the promise of being a compassionate conservative when he's neither. Bush and the Republicans are willing to use the rhetoric of responsibility and community, even though they don't believe a word of it and never do anything to create it, because they recognize that it's what most Americans want.

I think whether people live in a blue state or a red state, most of us want to live in the kind of society that exists in Vermont—where people take care of one another and where both parties acknowledge that government has obligations to ordinary people. Most important, we recognize that we have obligations to one another. Most people want to live in a society where the government ensures not just equal rights but equal opportunities: for decent health care, good public education, the ability to live to old age in comfort and serenity. But most Americans don't think it's possible.

It is possible. *We can* shrink the wealth gap. Build the middle class. Get health care for everyone. Provide funds to help families pay for college. Have decent public education. Other industrialized countries have done these things. So can we.

We can bridge racial and ethnic differences.

We can build a different kind of country, where we all recognize our mutual humanity and our obligation to one another as Americans, no matter what group we come from or what our background is. We can build a society where we acknowledge our common bonds and where respect means we don't expect people to live in the street and eat out of Dumpsters, a society where we can expect that people will be considered for who and not what they are.

We can bring people hope.

But for all of this we need real leaders, with a new way of talking about the issues. We need a new brand of politics. And a new brand of politicians.

★ 5 ★

Is Real Leadership Possible?

Bill Clinton once told me, "The American people will always vote for someone who is strong and wrong before they'll choose someone who is weak and right."

I think that's true.

Although I was often criticized during the campaign for coming on strongly, I think Americans desperately want a president who will clearly, forcefully, and unambiguously state their case. George W. Bush's greatest strength, despite being wrong on virtually every issue of long-term importance to the country, is that he always speaks with conviction in defending his policies.

For Democrats to offer voters a significant change over the long term, we need to say what we mean and not be afraid of the consequences. But there is a price to be paid for candor, as I and others inclined to speak our minds have discovered the hard way. There is no reward now in politics for saying what you think. On the contrary, in the get-along-go-along world of Washington, politicians are penalized for saying what they believe, and insincerity is the currency of the culture. (After I finished my campaign, I finally understood what Harry Truman had meant when he said, "If you want a friend in Washington, get a dog.")

America's politicians attack one another by day and slap one another on the back by evening. They can play this game because they know that their fighting words have no real meaning. And the media play right along, reporting on the game as though it were a story of substance. Indeed, the game becomes the story, and discussions of substance are relegated to a newspaper's inside pages if they are covered at all.

What passes for news are stories of little lasting importance. My candor—like John McCain's in a previous election—was covered as a personality trait. We both endured "temperament" stories—and the issues we were candid about took a backseat. Candor ended up being a vulnerability for us as much as it was a virtue.

Now, I am one of the least objective people in America when it comes to the media. My relationship with the press during the campaign was generally poor. Because of that, I realize now, I helped the media create a person who didn't exist. I was characterized as "angry and dark, even surly"—as one magazine put it.[1] I was said to be a person who suffered from panic attacks. I was said to have changed my position on the Iraq war. I was made out to be a draft dodger. All this wasn't merely the work of the media, however, or of the combustible mixture of my personality with the media. It was also an effect of spin.

Most people outside politics don't realize how it is that presidential-campaign press operations work. A campaign's press staff has two jobs: to make their candidate look good, and to make the other candidates look bad without letting their own candidates appear negative or unpleasant. Every day campaign press people called "spinners" call up reporters "on background" or off the record and try to sell them a positive story about their candidate or, more often, a negative story about another candidate, since that is usually of more interest to the reporters. It's a numbers game. A spinner may call twenty reporters to get one of them to write a story; if he succeeds—especially if a reporter from a major newspaper buys it—the other reporters will be pressured to get on the bandwagon the next day. If the spinner strikes paydirt, his version of the facts may become the story of the day, or even of the week, by getting amplified in the echo chamber of cable news stations (which have three hours' worth of real news to fill twenty-four hours' worth of programs) and embellished by pundits barking at one another all day and all night long. By the time the public sees the story through the eyes of reporters or pundits, the fingerprints of the people who spun the story have long since been wiped away. The story becomes fact, if only by repetition into "common knowledge."

All this is fine if your campaign is doing the spinning, but not so fine if you're a member of the public trying to learn something about candidates from the media and getting nothing but spin. It's also not so great if you're the target of all that spin. When I was the front-runner, I was the target of five Democratic spinners and one Republican spinner. Every day.

I've often thought back on something Gary Hart once told me: There is no such thing as a wimp who gets elected president of the United States. Campaigning in this atmosphere makes you necessarily tough. The question is, does it serve the country well?

Whether a story is true, partly true, or false makes little difference once the spin cycle begins. Most news organizations do not want to be embarrassed by putting out false information. But even worse would be to lose a ratings war or be beaten to a story that might be true. A prime example of the good and the bad is a story about a state trooper who for years provided my security when I was governor. He was fired as a result of events surrounding his admission of involvement in domestic abuse. The spinner story was that I had knowingly covered this up.

This story first surfaced when a local Republican got it on television in my 2000 reelection campaign. It had no particular effect on my reelection, since it was completely false. Then, in 2003, Vermont Republicans hoping to curry favor with the Bush folks tried to peddle the story again to Felix Schein of NBC. He turned down the story after going to Vermont and seeing it for what it was.

So Brian Ross of ABC used it.

And on it went.

One of my first experiences of being caught in a full-blown media maelstrom came in the spring of 2003, when John Kerry's then press spinner, Chris Lehane (who subsequently parted company from the campaign), called *The Boston Globe* because he'd found an article in the *Aspen Times* that said I'd spent a year after college living in Aspen and skiing. Lehane, who has built his reputation as the spinner of all spinners by cultivating reporters over late-night drinks and softly bending them to his will, got the *Globe* to write a story saying that although I'd been deferred from the draft for medical reasons, I'd been well enough to spend the next year pounding the bumps in Aspen. The story was written to sound as though I were a draft dodger and the medical deferment had been manufactured. The truth was, I had a low draft number, and I had a chronic back problem that still bothers me today. I had brought it to the army's attention, along with X rays, at my draft physical.

That the army refused to take me because of my back condition is not in dispute. But what the *Globe* did at Lehane's insistence was to make it sound as if I'd been dishonest with the army. The newspaper went on a fishing expedition: Why had I brought my X rays to the draft physical, anyway? "Dean was classified IY, according to military records," the story said, "meaning he was exempt from service for the duration of the war and free to head to Colorado after his Yale graduation, where he skied at Aspen and poured concrete.[2]

The story ricocheted all over the country afterward. Rick Lyman of *The New York Times* did a profile of me, and during a meeting with my mother in her New York apartment, he brought up the issue. My mother is as blunt and outspoken as I am. Yes, she laughed with Lyman, it's easy to see how that could look bad. But, she added, that is the peculiar nature of the condition, spondylolisthesis; it causes pain in certain situations—like when I have to sit or run or walk for a long time—but not in others.

Lyman laughed with her. He was a skilled interviewer, and I'd given him access to my whole family. He charmed them, he was nice to them, he wheedled them. "Yes, that looks bad," my mother said, "but that's the nature of the condition."

My mother ended up being quoted in the *Times* about her son's draft deferment: "Yeah, that looks bad."[3] When the campaign saw the story on the Internet, we called Lyman, who after some convincing agreed to make changes for the paper's next edition. But it was too late. By that time, the story was all over the United States in the national edition of *The New York Times,* which closes early.

• • •

Lyman is an example of the kind of reporter who, from a politician's point of view, is the most dangerous: pleasant, even a little bit obsequious. He's the kind of reporter who gains your confidence with lengthy and sympathetic interviews, only to write a far different portrayal from what you ever thought possible. I'd given Lyman free access to my family on the advice of a friendly reporter from the *Los Angeles Times* who had told me that the best way to handle the press was to give them as much access as they wanted so the relationship would be good. Unfortunately, I made the mistake of taking that advice, at least for a few days.

This kind of "quote massaging" happens over and over again. It was what led Jim VandeHei of *The Washington Post* to diagnose me with panic attacks: I'd been talking on the campaign plane about my brother Charlie, whose remains had just been discovered in Laos. I said that I'd been in therapy twenty-three years earlier to work through some issues I had regarding his death. Someone asked what made me go to therapy. I said, "I had panic attacks." Then the doctor in me rushed to make a correction because I hadn't actually suffered from panic attacks—which are accompanied by a whole slew of often terrifying physical symptoms—but really from something more akin to run-of-the-mill anxiety. I said so to the reporters. The next day, I read in *The Washington Post* that I had "panic attacks"[4]— valuable fodder for my political opponents, who, to their credit, never used it.

We asked Jim the next day, "How could you put that in the story?" He said, "My editor made me do it."

In an interview on foreign policy with *Time* magazine, I expressed my view that refusing to engage with other countries diplomatically would end up weakening us militarily. We wouldn't always have the strongest military in the world, I said, if we failed to understand that diplomacy was an important weapon in our arsenal. The stringer I spoke with sent in his file, and the editors incorporated it into a longer story that ended on my words: "We won't always have the strongest military."[5] This remark was picked up by the spinners for all the other campaigns—and disseminated by a host of other media outlets—as an example of how I wanted America to be a second-class military power.

The press's tendency to run with partial quotes, misleading quotes, and nonquotes was part of the reason—along with the susceptibility of the press corps to my opponents' spinners—that I became known for making so many gaffes. While few individual stories held up under scrutiny, the constant drumbeat did hurt us, and it played into our opponents' hands in Iowa.

I didn't mind the gaffe stories quite as much as the ones that were entirely made up. *Newsweek*'s Michael Isikoff, for example, pursued a story that I had participated in insider trading, and *The Boston Globe* printed a story intimating that I'd had a secret meeting with Enron over a captive insurance company (which Enron didn't own until a year after the supposed secret meeting).[6] Both stories died of their own ridiculousness, but not before they'd been picked up by the national media.

These stories were silly, and the impression they created was completely false. But once they started to circulate (not coincidentally, around the time that Al Gore endorsed me), they seemed to come on in an avalanche. Sometimes they were the work of the spinners in other campaigns. That didn't seem so bad; after all, the campaign press people were just doing their jobs. More insulting was when reporters ran with scurrilous stories, based on rumor and innuendo, without even checking the facts. They knew that some juicy stories were too good to check—so they didn't.

Even after the campaign was over, they had trouble stopping. In March 2004 a story came out that I was embarrassing the Kerry campaign with my continued gaffes. This originated from a press-conference call that the Kerry people had asked me to do. I'd been talking about how wrong President Bush's Iraq policies were and how as a result a number of terrible things had happened, like the train bombing in Spain that killed more than two hundred people. I was asked: "Are you blaming President Bush for that?" I said of course I was not. I blamed the terrorists and simply noted that in a note they'd left for investigators, the terrorists themselves had made the link between Spain's presence in Iraq and their attack on Spanish soil.

After that, the Republicans issued a statement claiming

that I'd blamed President Bush for the bombing in Spain. The press ran straight back to Kerry and confronted him with my "statement," not identifying its source as the Republican National Committee. Kerry, of course, said he couldn't agree with what I'd said. So the reporters on Kerry's bus wrote a story about how I was causing the prospective nominee heartburn. . . .

To the credit of the media, good reporting can crowd out the bad.

I was in Washington for a convention of newspaper editors on the day the United States invaded Iraq. When I came out of the meeting, Ron Brownstein of the *Los Angeles Times* ambushed me: "Now that our troops are in Iraq, what should we do?"

Ron is a well-respected political reporter. I answered his question directly, saying that I didn't think we had any choice other than to support our troops. Now that they were in Iraq, they'd have to stay there until we got them out in an orderly way. American credibility was on the line. We couldn't pull them out after one day and put ourselves and our soldiers in danger; we were stuck. I repeated that I thought the president had made a terrible mistake.

Brownstein went off and wrote an article saying that I, with every other Democratic contender in the presidential race, had "quickly lined up behind President Bush's decision to attack Iraq."[7] My press people picked it up off the Internet that night, before the paper went to bed. I called Brownstein to protest. He refused to change his story. Then he stopped taking my calls. So I called his editor. My press people went crazy. The candidate himself calling an editor! I was told: Don't you ever do that again. It only makes things worse, they said, which was probably true.

The story ran unchanged the next day with the headline DEMOCRATIC HOPEFULS RALLY BEHIND BUSH. Fortunately, Nedra Pickler of the Associated Press had been outside the conference, too. She wrote a story that accurately relayed to the American people what I'd said, and because her story contradicted Brownstein's, his wasn't picked up as widely as it might have been.[8] But that didn't stop him or writers like *The Washington Post*'s Jim VandeHei from later going to town on the "news" that I'd started to "throw voters some curves" and flip-flop on my key positions.[9] (Fortunately, I'd already gotten some good advice from Bill Clinton: "You don't have to worry about what the *Post* says," he told me early in my campaign. "Nobody outside the Beltway ever reads it." In fact, he said—in what was one of the most valuable warnings I ever received—"Don't read anything written inside the Beltway at all. It'll only make you mad and demoralize your staff.")

My favorite press story came about two months after the campaign was over, when *The New York Times* decided to do a story on the bizarre practice of shooting fish in Vermont (a sport permitted only here and in the state of Virginia). They called my office to ask for comment. Needless to say, this was a back-burner issue for me. I'd never been a great fan of pickerel—the big, long, ugly-looking good-for-nothing fish with huge teeth that's the most common target—but I wasn't sure anyone really needed to go around shooting them, either. Most people in Vermont feel pretty similarly—if they think about the issue at all. In fact, our legislature has been on the verge of taking up the subject of fishing by rifle for as long as I can remember.

I happened to be busy working on this book on the day that *The New York Times* called and not particularly inclined to turn over staff resources for digging through records to find my official position from back when I'd been governor. And so, when the phone calls redoubled and the threats began ("This is going to be a really big deal. We're going to put the governor's refusal to comment on page one"), I ignored them.

"I'm not going to do your research for you," said my loyal press assistant. "Look it up."

A few weeks later, the story ran on page one. It included the pertinent information that "the issue is apparently so touchy that Howard Dean, governor from 1991 to 2003, 'has no interest in going on the record on that subject. . . .' "

As troublesome as its sins of commission are the media's errors of omission. In July 2004, long after John Kerry had clinched the nomination, a number of my supporters asked me why he wasn't saying much about the war or jobs. I had been out on the road with John, campaigning in battleground states, and I'd seen him do a great job on the war in front of four thousand people in Portland, Oregon. He did even better the next day at an unemployment round table. He was compassionate, empathetic, organized, and concise. He was terrific. The local press corps gave him a nice write-up. The national press hardly wrote anything at all.

In fairness, you can't write the same story thirty days in a row if you're a national reporter for a media outlet covering the campaign. But candidates have to give the same speech and perform the same way day after day after day, because they're facing a new audience day after day after day. The result is that if you don't live in one of the seventeen or twenty battleground states in this election, you think Kerry isn't addressing the big issues, since you see the campaign through the lens of reporters and their editors, who really aren't interested in what's happening on the ground. Once a story like "Kerry is avoiding the issues" starts to Ping-Pong, it takes on a life of its own.

I genuinely liked most of the reporters who traveled with us during the campaign. Our plane often featured marathon games of hearts or "Oh Hell" with off-the-record language from both reporters and candidates that made Dick Cheney's recent Senate-floor remarks sound like *Mother Goose*. I don't think the reporting on my campaign cost me the nomination. We peaked too early, and we made enough mistakes to be responsible for losing ourselves. Still, what I saw on the campaign trail left me with the lasting impression that there's something very wrong with the American media today.

• • •

A reporter on the campaign plane once accused me of being contemptuous of the press. Even though I denied it, she and I both knew it was true.

I think the media is a failing institution. The most common problem—and it is almost always deliberate, as Jim VandeHei's slip in blaming his editor for the "panic attack" reference indicated—is that reporters are under enormous pressure from editors to write what the editors think is a good story rather than what reporters actually see or hear. And editors are under enormous pressure from publishers who are under enormous pressure from CEOs who are under enormous pressure from shareholders. It isn't sloppy reporters who are the ultimate culprits, although they are the recipients of most Americans' ire with the media.

The truth is, reporters are rewarded for twisting facts to make them fit the story line of the day. I have had reporters tell me with specific illustrations that they are even encouraged to concoct stories by stringing together facts that aren't related. The Jayson Blairs and Jack Kelleys of the world (reporters who were dismissed from *The New York Times* and *USA Today*, respectively, for submitting stories that they fabricated) are not aberrations; they are outliers. They are the products of too much pressure to produce, and of a newsroom culture that takes both financial and editorial shortcuts to avoid the psychologically and financially costly hard work it takes to do what Bob Woodward and Carl Bernstein did thirty years ago in bringing down the president of the United States by uncovering the Watergate scandal.

Reporters get taught by editors, publishers, and CEOs that excitement sells, and like many in my profession—medicine—these mentors have divided loyalties. With the advent of HMOs came pressure on doctors from insurance companies to watch the bottom line, an aspect of medicine that today is ubiquitous. It began to happen while I was still practicing medicine; for many doctors it is now part of daily life. They are constantly reminded that they are expected to have divided loyalties, to shareholders as well as patients. While most doctors don't knowingly succumb to that pressure, it works, and medical decisions don't always favor patients over shareholders.

I think the same thing has been going on in newsrooms for quite some time.

The reason there are no new Woodwards and Bernsteins today is that there are not many Ben Bradlees left, and there are not many media outlets left who would want a Bradlee—he was the *Washington Post* editor who not only trusted the judgment of two junior reporters in the face of enormous pressure to stop the Watergate investigation, but also paid these reporters for nearly two years with little initial gain. Months of investigation were required before there was any return on the investment for *The Washington Post*, and all the while, Nixon and his allies were hounding and threatening the owners and management of the *Post*, with potential costs such as loss of access and even economic consequences.

The consolidation of the media—bringing about a situation in which most Americans get their news from huge multinational corporations—has succeeded, where Nixon's forces failed. Serious investigative reporting has been brought to a halt.

The other big change in the way the American media works has been wrought by Rupert Murdoch. In Murdoch's Australia and in much of Europe, it is accepted that media outlets are advocates not only of points of view but of political parties themselves. Most parties have newspapers they consider their own. In fact, the right-wing prime minister of Italy, Silvio Berlusconi, actually owns his own media empire in addition to controlling the supposedly neutral state-run television network. Given this example, it is not surprising, as Robert Greenwald's documentary *Outfoxed* showed so brilliantly, that Fox, the *New York Post*, and Murdoch's other properties in America are advocates for the Republican Party.

Tradition in the United States is that media outlets may lean liberal or conservative, but keep their news coverage separate from their editorial policy. That tradition is now honored only occasionally. *The Wall Street Journal,* for example, is a well-written middle-of-the-road newspaper, despite the fact that its editorial board seems to comprise people who are taking dictation from Tom DeLay and Karl Rove. My hometown paper, on the other hand, never wrote an editorial in two years about the state's most heated controversy in a century—the passage of the civil unions bill giving gay and lesbian Vermonters the same rights as everyone else—because the conservative publisher refused to allow the paper to take the position that the rest of the editorial board wanted to write about.

The real problem with the influence that Rupert Murdoch has on the media in America is not the disingenuousness of Fox News's "fair and balanced" slogan. The real problem is that Murdoch hires people who are very good at what they do. (I say this despite the *New York Post*'s July 2004 headline proclaiming KERRY'S CHOICE: DEM PICKS GEPHARDT AS VP CANDIDATE.)

Roger Ailes, who runs Fox News, has devised a snappy format with terrific graphics that are appealing to younger viewers. The program does dumb down the news and is more than occasionally misleading. In fact, a study last year by the Program on International Policy Attitudes—a research center affiliated with the University of Maryland's School of Public Affairs—showed that heavy viewers of the Fox News Channel were four times as likely to hold erroneous views about the war in Iraq as were viewers of PBS and listeners of NPR.[10] But despite this, Fox has managed to earn the best ratings in cable television. Their prime-time network shows are equally well done. It's not surprising, then, that the corporations that own Fox's rivals have put pressure on their news divisions to become more like Fox. And they have done so.

• • •

The real cost of media consolidation and Foxification in our time is not, as many of my supporters believe, censorship, although that sometimes happens (witness the removal of the popular band the Dixie Chicks from 250 Cumulus-owned radio stations after the lead singer criticized President Bush over Iraq). The real danger is that, in the pursuit of entertainment and ratings, the role of the media in our democracy has been trivialized.

A free society depends on a vigilant media. The American media, obsessed with quarterly profits and full of reporters trained to produce stories that are entertaining rather than substantive, are not doing what democracy depends on: getting the story right. Some senior newspaper people believe that this problem was accelerated by the Monica Lewinsky scandal, after which reporters who specialized in scandalmongering became stars and real investigative reporting became a lost art. Consequently, this theory goes, the press corps was unprepared to deal with issues like 9/11, the Halliburton-Cheney relationship and the Bush administration's misleading statements leading up to the Iraq war. Reporters had been led to believe that their advancement depended upon their ability to create sensationalist stories rather than their willingness to find and develop substantive ones.

Many Americans under age thirty get their news from *The Daily Show* or from the Internet. That means the next generation to lead America does not regard *The New York*

Times as any more authoritative than the Internet postings of a conspiracy theorist. I remember all my civics classes in which the teachers stressed that the purpose of education in America was to learn critical thinking, so we could evaluate all sources and then come to a reasonable conclusion. Now that a new generation is coming to the news without editors to choose what's newsworthy, we are about to test how well that concept works on a national scale.

Still, there is hope. First of all, there still are outstanding journalists who work every day to get it right. Being human, they don't always succeed, but neither do doctors, police officers, or politicians. Dan Balz of *The Washington Post* and Mike Glover and Nedra Pickler of the Associated Press are some of them. And much to my surprise, I came away from the campaign with real admiration for Tom Brokaw, Peter Jennings, and Dan Rather, the anchors for NBC, ABC, and CBS, respectively. They seem to me to represent the Walter Cronkite school of journalism, where getting it right and newsworthiness are more important than speed and entertainment value.

Which brings us to the discussion you all have been waiting for—the "Scream Speech."

In June 2004, I surprised the National Association of Broadcasters by telling them that this iconic campaign event, replayed on television more than seven hundred times in one week, never happened. The association members were stunned. After all, they had all seen it. On television.

But the Scream never did happen. Not the way most Americans saw it, anyway.

After we came in a distant third in Iowa, I felt that I needed to go out and rev up the troops, including twelve hundred mostly young people who had traveled from such distant places as Alaska and Hawaii (and even, in the case of one expat, from Japan) to knock on doors for us in the middle of an Iowa winter. Most of my advisers agreed with me. Perhaps it was the wrong decision. If I could do it again, I'd bear in mind that the whole nation was watching and that I needed to think of addressing those outside the room as well as those present. But I didn't think of this then. I'm a loyal person, and I thought these folks who'd worked so hard for me, for so many months, needed a tough, upbeat speech.

The room was explosive. There was so much cheering and yelling that the speech I gave couldn't be heard by anyone except those onstage.

At the time, the traveling press corps thought my speech seemed like a lot of speeches I've given, typically high-energy. Needless to say, they were amazed, then, to be the recipients of nasty queries from their editors the following morning asking how they could have missed the big story of Dean's meltdown.

How did the editors "see" something the reporters missed? What happened was this: As is always true for pool footage, the microphone recording me had been set up in such a way that ambient crowd noise wasn't picked up at all. The TV cameras feeding out to the editors (and viewers) back home did not show the crowd around me (at least the snippets that were rebroadcast did not). So I looked like a crazy man, laughing and shouting to myself and the people behind me. Big news, no doubt. Even bigger entertainment.

Ten days after the speech, Diane Sawyer from ABC News took the trouble to figure out what had really happened. Peter Jennings did a nice story explaining how the Scream had come into being. But the cable networks kept playing it. And the late-night comics had a field day. It was, indeed, pure entertainment.

I didn't lose the nomination because of the Iowa speech; John Kerry locked it up that night by winning. And I don't think the speech cost me much in the long run, since I went on to win the same number of primaries as John Edwards and Wes Clark. But the Iowa Scream provided a classic example of how things can go wrong in American journalism. All the elements were there: the repetition of a misleading story, the incessant replays as entertainment, the willingness of editors on television and print desks to override what a reporter tells them from the field if the story they want to use is more entertaining than the truth.

If the network anchors and a few principled reporters can't stem the tide, where do we turn for hope of change? First, of course, is to do what America's young people do: bypass the mainstream media by using the Internet to get the news directly from the horse's mouth—and, of course, *The Daily Show*. That'll have the effect of using the marketplace's power to adjust how the mainstream media gives us news. We can also rely on National Public Radio, whose listenership has doubled in the last ten years as commercial radio stations were acquired by big corporations and dropped news programming.

The other ray of hope is local news, which is generally more open, less cynical, less slick, and more fact oriented than what the national media produces.

When I was governor of Vermont, I had my ups and downs with the local media. But my relationship with the press corps was based on a kind of mutual respect. I liked most of the people who covered me. The press corps was small, everyone knew each other, and they knew their readers. There was a kind of professional mechanism of self-correction that went on within the community. If a reporter took a particularly hard advocacy role on an issue and tried to pass it off as news, it wouldn't really fly. If someone got something wrong in a local paper, it would be corrected—not necessarily as prominently as it might be, but it wouldn't be repeated afterward, either.

I did have some bad experiences: notably right before

the gubernatorial election in 2000, when a reporter for the state's biggest television station—which happens to be owned by a major Republican campaign contributor—led the news with a story about an allegedly dubious position I had taken on a free-speech issue. He went on, "But here's one kind of free speech the governor doesn't seem to object to." Then he showed a picture of protesters burning an American flag, in an apparent reference to my concern over the free-speech issues raised by a proposed constitutional amendment to ban flag burning. This was pretty awful, but when we complained, the anchor agreed to run a correction and an apology the next night, in the same spot on the evening news lineup. The story died.

When I returned home after a year and a half on the road, a couple of the most respected members of the Vermont media told me incredible stories about how their national affiliates had repeatedly insisted upon running stories that they knew weren't true. For example, the Vermont media knew the "Enron meeting" story was a joke. They knew about the "insider trading" story because I had brought it to their attention nine years before. In the case of the Associated Press, reporters told my press staff that they were ordered by their New York– and Washington-based superiors to do research on stories they knew in advance didn't hold water. What the Vermonters particularly couldn't believe was that the national reporters ran with stories even after they'd been told by the local reporters who knew me best that the stories were wrong.

Local people trust local news far more than national news for a good reason. Local reporters in many small markets are doing a much better job serving the public, the country, and democracy right now than are their better-paid and higher-status colleagues in New York and Washington. It seems a pity that so many local reporters around the country envy the national press corps and hope to join it. I hope that, in the future, local press outlets will try harder to keep their best reporters home and pay them better so it's worth it for them to stay.

This is a particularly perilous time to govern in America. Our budget deficits are enormous. Our corporate and personal debt loads are enormous. We're one crisis of confidence away from a really serious economic problem. This means that all four branches of our government—the three elected ones and the one unelected watchdog—will have to do a far better job in the future, if our country is going to maintain its status as the preeminent military, economic, and moral leader of the world.

Anyone who's willing to try to be a real leader in the coming years will have to make some very tough decisions and be willing to stand up for some potentially unpopular policies. We'll have to get a handle on the economy, rebalance the budget, and keep it balanced. We'll have to negotiate new free-trade agreements that will better protect workers and the environment as well as our national security.

It will require guts to go up against the supporters of sugarcoated tax cuts who won't be straightforward with the American people about their true costs. This will require a willingness to stand up for what's right and take a lot of heat from the corporate community, who will not want to see those trade agreements or those tax policies changed. It will also mean talking tough to the American people, who must be convinced that our country's long-term health depends on making hard choices and setting budget priorities now.

If we are to move toward universal health coverage, in particular, Americans will have to accept one basic truth: You can't bring everything to everyone. We will have to make choices and set priorities. Every other nation that provides its citizens with basic health coverage (read: every other industrialized nation in the world) does this. They address it through some form of health-care "rationing." We do this in the United States, too. We ration by price and, if you live in a rural area or an inner city, availability. But we don't have universal access.

In an ideal world, we could have everything. But we don't live in an ideal world, and acting as though we do is the best way to guarantee that we will never bring change to the real world. If the Democrats are going to bring health coverage to all Americans in the early decades of the twenty-first century, we'll have to show our mettle as leaders and be willing to talk to people about stark choices and not so pleasant issues, like how it's not only the insurance companies, drug companies, lawyers, doctors, and hospitals that are responsible for health-care costs. It's also we patients who expect all possible services but don't want to pay for them. And it's the business community, where the same people who complain about health-care costs as employers vote for big local hospital expansions as hospital trustees.

We'll never have real leaders who say what they mean if we don't have a press corps willing and able to hold politicians and themselves accountable for their words and actions. We'll never have leaders willing to tell the truth if we don't have a press corps willing to write it. *And an electorate who's willing to hear it.*

When I was governor and I had bad news to give, I'd call a press conference and deliver the bad news and not get defensive about it. That's what I had learned to do as a doctor. It does no good to be defensive or evasive about the fact that somebody has cancer; you have to be supportive. You have to move on from the bad news to figure out your plan of action for a cure. In politics, I've learned, as in the doctor's office, there's an advantage to telling people the unpleasant truth straightaway. It gives you the opportunity to act before it's too late. It also helps people put their faith in you when you propose new ways of doing things. That's why I'm so intolerant of politicians like President Bush who won't take responsibility for delivering bad news. By keeping painful information from us, they take away our possibility to find a cure.

As governor, I went head-to-head with the liberal members of my own party in order to pay off our deficit. I made a lot of enemies on my own side when I cut tax rates in order to attract businesses and their jobs to Vermont. I succeeded because I put my legislature in a position where they had to go along with me after I'd patiently explained again and again to the people of our state why things had to be done the way I thought.

My deficit-busting and growth measures ultimately gave the state's Independents and moderate Republicans confidence in me. Later on, when we started working on things like civil unions and school funding redistribution, many of them stuck with me because they knew I wouldn't waste their money and I would deliver bad news if I had to. When we did universal health care for kids, they stuck with me, too, because they knew it wouldn't be a big, wasteful social program. They knew they could trust me to manage their money and that I would tell the truth as I understood it, so they signed on for expanded social programs.

Countries do well if they're run well. Basically, they have to be run like a good family business. If America is run with long-term thoughtfulness about fiscal balance and responsibility while making long-term social investments in small children and their families, investors from all over the world will be drawn to us. If America continues to be run with no holds barred on spending and inadequate taxation, then the job-creating community will know that our fiscal situation is in decline, and there'll be no likelihood of recovery in the future. American leaders won't think long-term, however, until the press rewards them for doing so.

Democracy doesn't fix itself. Budget deficits, debt, the division and disenfranchisement of the American people—none of that will fix itself. Which is why we need leaders who will lead and media watchdogs that will look out for Americans' best interests. Since corporations are not equipped to do this because of their fiduciary responsibility to shareholders, we ought to reverse the FCC policies we have seen since the Reagan years.

The start of the remedy should be policies that discourage large corporations from ownership of media; restore limits on media ownership in individual markets; require a return to the local equal-time rule; and require the users of the airwaves owned by the public to provide airtime to multiple points of view at election time as part of a package of true campaign-finance reform. Then the media will begin to return to their essential role as guardians and watchdogs in our democracy and will enable real leadership in the political world to become the rule rather than the exception.

★ 6 ★

Democracy: A User's Manual

The blueprint for the renewal of the Democratic Party is simple. It's not enough to elect a Democratic president, or to constrain our outlook to one that is simply election-to-election.

This is a mistake we've made in the past. The right wing has been able to take over the three branches of our government because they've implemented a long-term, disciplined plan. We need now to do the same.

There will be considerable assets left over in November from the Kerry campaign, the Democratic House and Senate campaigns, and the Dean for America campaign. These assets include a vast voter file compiled by millions of face-to-face visits, a huge small-donor base, thousands of trained canvassers, and various training organizations. We have to make sure those assets are coordinated and used long after the election.

The Republicans did this twenty years ago to great effect: by developing a serious, coordinated approach to establishing a permanent election-to-election presence on the American political scene through think tanks, foundations, and grassroots organizations. People such as the anti-tax crusader Grover Norquist started holding regular meetings to talk about how to spread the right wing's message. The Club for Growth, a far-right political action committee founded in 1999 to back hard-core conservative candidates against what it called RINOs—Republicans in Name Only—was so successful in identifying and mobilizing its rich anti-tax constituency that, after only three years of operation, it was able to raise over $10 million from nine thousand members for the midterm elections of 2002.[1] These far-right organizations have shown us how tough you have to be in fighting for a permanent presence on the national political stage. There's no reason moderate and progressive Democrats can't fight back using the same tactics. To do that, we have to be organized, and our organization has to be sustained. We can't think just from election to election. We need to build a forward-thinking, long-term presence in the states, in grassroots organizations, in think tanks and foundations, on the Internet, and over the airwaves so that our own smart and honest "noise machine" can plug into the conversations going on in the American electorate.

We have to rebuild our grassroots organization.
The Democratic Party has ignored its grass roots for the

past twenty years, in terms of both raising money for local candidates and supporting and finding new local office-holders.

What typically has happened at the state level is that if there's a Democratic governor, the state Democratic Party becomes a reelection machine for the governor and doesn't do much—unless the governor is very party-building-minded—to help local officeholders. If there's a Republican governor, things are twice as difficult. The state Democratic Party has no governor to help raise money, and there isn't much extra money to help nourish the grass roots.

The same thing happens on the national level. When you have a Democratic president, the Democratic National Committee is dedicated to reelecting that president. The Democratic Senatorial Campaign Committee and the Democratic Congressional Campaign Committee are dedicated to reelecting their senators and representatives. The party structure works fine for the people at the top, but office-holders at the bottom—the people like state representatives, county commissioners, and county clerks, who have the closest ties to voters—are on their own. They generally don't get the kind of support from the state or national party that they need in order to campaign effectively and win elections. This neglect of our grass roots is something we really have to change.

We have to change our understanding of grassroots organizing as well. We learned during the campaign that a grassroots organization really has to be a two-way effort. Because we started out with no money and a lot of enthusiastic grassroots activists, we quickly ceded power to local folks and let them run things in their area as they saw fit. This turned out to be the single most important innovation in political campaigning that the Dean for America campaign discovered, and it is the only one that hasn't been picked up by any of the other campaigns, either Republican or Democrat. Everything else—the small-donor programs, the house parties, the Internet organizing, the interactive websites—has been copied. The most critical piece hasn't been, because it requires a cognitive change in those who run campaigns and not just a change in technique or technology.

Letting go of central control in campaigns is what gives the electorate—particularly activists—real power. I learned this by doing it. When I used the phrase "You have the power," I didn't at first realize the full impact of what I was saying. I meant only that Americans, through working together to change America, could overcome the forces of the right wing and reassume their constitutional role in running the country.

What I didn't understand was that "You have the power" was a lot more than a rhetorical phrase. It didn't apply only to people's power to change the country; it also applied to their ability to direct a campaign. In my campaign, people at the grassroots level made decisions about how everything worked. They decided where to leaflet and what the leaflets would say. They organized and ran hundreds of organizations like African-Americans for Dean, Latinos for Dean, Punx for Dean, Irish-Americans for Dean, and others, which sprang up, not from a central "oureach" desk in Burlington but spontaneously all over the country. All we had to do, after we unleashed this creativity, was weave the organizations into a central campaign that sometimes was more of a clearinghouse than it was a control-and-command organization.

The idea of a decentralized campaign terrifies most politicians who have grown used to giving out their ideas and letting others respond. It initially made me a little nervous, too, but, in truth, we had no choice. We had no money or name recognition at first; all we had was a willingness to fight back.

I soon learned to trust the grass roots. They did occasionally get way out there and do things that turned out to be problems (for example, you can't call the president of the United States a fascist), but most of the time, these remarkable Americans who had often never been involved in politics, and certainly never in a presidential campaign, not only got it right, they taught us a lot about what was going on in the rest of the country.

The great genius of our campaign was that we were willing to listen.

"I am the youth vote," wrote Traci Carpenter, a student at Michigan State University, in the July 12 issue of *Newsweek*. "And I'm tired of being preached at, studied, and wooed. . . . I am neither lazy nor apathetic. I'm confused and frustrated. I am told to care about issues like Social Security and health care, when chances are high that I won't even find a job after I graduate from college. I juggle low-wage, part-time jobs or a full-time class schedule, and I'm not necessarily available on Nov. 2. . . . Howard Dean tried to change my mind about the political process. He made me a part of his campaign, rather than a target. He recognized the power I hold, rather than ignoring my potential."[2]

When I read that I thought: *What are the Democrats waiting for?* Here's a college senior providing us with the blueprint for winning elections again. It's time to wake up—and to realize that the way to unlock the power of the electorate is to acknowledge that the voters are the ones who have the power and to treat them that way.

Without the involvement and commitment of people at the ground level, you don't really have a party. You have no pool from which to draw future congresspeople, senators, and presidents. And you have no genuine excitement. The truth is, nourishing the grass roots is helpful for the people who are running for president or the House or the Senate. Suppose someone decides to run for school board and puts together a little operation with twenty or thirty supporters helping out. Let's say those people then mobilize a thousand people to vote in the school board election who otherwise wouldn't have thought much about it and maybe wouldn't have voted at all. Those people aren't going to skip the presidential ballot. If they've been brought in by our people, they're not going to vote for a right-wing Republican. They'll vote for a progressive Democrat. That's one reason why focusing on the grass roots is good for the party. Another reason is that nourishing the grass roots keeps ordinary people active, interested in policy, and involved in political campaigns. This really matters—because the tragedy of the Democratic Party in the last twenty years has been that its constituents got to a point where they didn't care anymore. The Republicans did a terrific job in this same period of mobilizing and energizing their grassroots base—particularly thanks to the organizational skills of Ralph Reed, who made his Christian Coalition a powerful organizing tool for the party and cemented its ideological hold on the Republican base.

When I talk about the importance of nourishing the grass roots, I'm talking about something much larger than a mere organizing strategy. I'm talking about building a community, locally and nationally. We saw this concept demonstrated dramatically during my presidential campaign as we tracked the spectacular order growth of our declared supporters online. The people who supported us on the Internet (and they numbered, let's remember, more than seven hundred thousand by the campaign's end) weren't isolated individuals writing in to our blog or sending in their five- and ten-dollar donations. They were a community—people with common interests who found one another and bonded. (Two supporters have since written me that they met their future spouses through the on-line campaign.)

There is a stereotype about the type of people who form online communities: that they're a self-selected group of smart people who are reasonably well educated and feel somewhat alienated from the society around them. They go to work, they have jobs, but they are often more comfortable interacting on a personal level via the Internet. In fact, the Internet community is far broader than that. I was stunned when I campaigned in Sun City, Arizona, and found that most of the seventy- to ninety-year-olds who had come to see me knew a lot about me from the Internet. The myth that African-Americans and Latinos don't use the Web much is also nonsense. It is a tool that is even more powerful than we imagine. The digital divide is getting smaller, and its potential for uniting people is growing exponentially.

Of course, the Internet alone is not enough. During my campaign, we had another fantastic opportunity to see a new sort of community building through our innovative system of house meetings. This was a form of grassroots organizing crafted for us by Marshall Ganz, a Harvard University sociologist who honed his techniques two decades ago working with the United Farm Workers in California. The house meetings were different from the traditional house parties candidates use to raise money. For those, people come together to socialize, receive a conference call at some point from the candidate, and afterward take out their checkbooks. Our house meetings drew together strangers with common interests and goals. Unlike traditional house parties, they weren't primarily about politics. They were, simply put, about meeting.

They'd start when our organizers—ordinary people who'd done some training with us on running these meetings—would share their life stories. Eventually they would tell how the events in their lives had led them to become involved with my campaign. A woman with a gay brother, for example, might say she'd been drawn to me when she read about my position on the civil unions issue. A man whose family had struggled to deal with health-care issues might talk about why he was drawn to my support for universal health coverage. Then everyone would tell his or her story. People would share their concerns, their hopes, their fears, their aspirations. They would bond as a group. And they would talk, above all, about the issues affecting their group, rather than about my campaign per se.

At the end of the meeting, the guests would be asked if they wanted to get involved in the campaign or organize their own house meetings. Inevitably, some would, and our local organization would spread. People who'd never taken charge of any kind of organization would find themselves acting as real leaders—organizing voter drives, phone banks, letter-writing campaigns. We'd give them real responsibility, and they'd rise time and again to the occasion. They wouldn't do it solely out of a sense of obligation to me, or of loyalty to my campaign, but out of loyalty to this new peer group they'd formed. They would support me out of a sense of obligation to their community. It was a remarkably powerful thing.

The very special thing about the house-meeting system was that it put people at the center of the grassroots campaign. Not issues, not fund-raising, but people and their feelings, their life stories, their personal experiences.

This matter of putting people at the center of a campaign flies in the face of the major trend in organizing and fund-raising followed by both major political parties: "data mining." In this practice, campaigns use massive electronic databases (the "data mart") that contain tons of consumer information to figure out individual voters' buying habits and, through a statistical model, their political inclinations. They find out where you shop, what you buy, what kind of car you drive, what sweaters you wear, and what magazines you read. Based on that information, they divide people into "buckets." There's a dark red bucket, a dark blue bucket, a light blue bucket, a light red bucket, and so on, depending on where people fall on the

Democratic-to-Republican spectrum. Campaigns then devise direct-mail programs based on which bucket a person falls into. It's a way of categorizing people without ever asking them a question.

This technique, which has been used more and more frequently over the past fifteen years, has done immeasurable damage to our grassroots efforts. Campaigns devised and run on marketing principles by political professionals have come at the expense of precinct captains and other community members who have connections to lots of other people. These folks have dropped out of the political process, which means that all the people they normally talk to have dropped out, too. Turning voters into consumer composites means that real people, until the moment they enter the voting booth, aren't part of the process at all. This means that they often don't even make it to the ballot box.

We have to put people back at the center of political campaigns. And we, as a party, must remember to stay centered on our traditional Democratic values, which are about people. The truth is, when you trade your values for the hope of winning, you end up losing and having no values—so you keep losing.

We have to reconnect with our base.

In recent years the Democrats, in our pursuit of big dollars, have neglected the people we're there to serve. We let our connection to our base atrophy and have forgotten, as they say in politics, who brought us to the dance. In service to a falsely named "centrism," we've sidestepped every major request from labor unions, especially on including worker protections in our free-trade agreements. We've made decisions and set policy to please the corporate interests that financed us, without thinking about what the long-term implications would be for ordinary Americans. The abandonment of labor has hurt middle-class people terribly. Globalization has occasioned an enormous race to the bottom in terms of workers' protections and benefits.

The labor unions are not strong or widespread enough in the American workforce to put the squeeze on our government to change current trade agreements. The Democrats have to do so, if we want to attract and keep the middle-class working people we seek to claim as our constituency. Being a centrist means balancing budgets, not abandoning American working people and the middle class.

The Democrats also need to smarten up on effectively reaching out to minority groups, African-Americans in particular. There's a new generation of African-American voters now who don't automatically vote Democratic because of what the party did for them back in the days of Lyndon Johnson or FDR. The way they see it, it's a brand-new day. They know perfectly well that we still haven't achieved racial equality in America. We still don't have equal opportunity. African-American kids still have a tougher time getting a decent education than do white kids. There's still a disproportionate allocation of resources away from schools with large populations of children of color. Americans haven't become color-blind in their hiring. And neither have the courts in their sentencing.

Democrats have made the mistake in recent years of thinking that if we go to African-American communities three weeks before an election and tell our local people they've got to get out the vote, they'll do it wholeheartedly, and everything will work out fine. The truth is—as we saw in the last midterm elections—you can't get out the vote unless people have a compelling reason to go out and vote, and what best compels them is the belief that you're going to make their lives better.

There's another piece of this. Our party, like the Republicans, has come to deal with members of minority groups not as individuals deserving of attention but as members of special-interest groups. This is foolish. Special-interest groups comprise people who are trying to get something out of the government in return for payments or special legislation. African-Americans and Jews and Latinos and Asian-Americans and women aren't special-interest groups. They are our people; they built the Democratic Party. Various groups of Americans may be principally affected by certain issues—like racial discrimination or immigration or abortion rights—but they, like all Americans, are basically in agreement on most of the things that are really important.

We Democrats must learn that people who happen to belong to the same racial or ethnic group aren't all the same. They have the same variety of opinions on political issues as the majority population. So if we're going to make a special pitch to the people who have traditionally been at the center of our base—people who happen to be part of the Jewish or African-American or Latino community— let's address them as Americans first and Latinos or Jews or African-Americans afterward.

Reconnecting with our grassroots leadership and our traditional base isn't the only key to reviving our party, however. We have to go further.

We have to take our message to people we don't normally talk to.

Since I ended my presidential campaign and started campaigning for others, I've found myself in conservative states like Texas, Mississippi, and Utah in addition to the closely divided battleground states. I do this because I believe that if we Democrats never go to places like these, then we're not a national party, and we can't expect to make converts in these Republican-leaning states. People there never get exposed to progressive Democratic values; the right-wingers can paint us any way they like if we don't show up and fight back.

Democrats should never cede a single state. That doesn't mean we have to pour money we don't have where we have no chance to win. But it does mean we have to build and nurture our grass roots in every single state, and we have to support them with campaign visits from national candidates for office. In the future, we have to be willing to go to conservative parts of the country where liberals and progressives have been afraid to go for many, many years and start talking about our issues again. Here's why: People in conservative areas around the country are going to wise up to the fact that Republicans never provide jobs. They never do anything for health care. They never do anything for education. We have to go to conservative parts of the country and show people that their interests are actually our interests and that these common interests of ours aren't being served by the Republicans.

If we're willing to go to some conservative states, we might not win the first or second election we compete in. But ultimately, we'll get out the message. We'll inevitably attract the attention of new voters. And sooner or later, voters are going to say, *Wait a minute. Maybe the Republicans have always been more my speed on race issues and gay marriage, but the truth is, for all the years they've been in office, I haven't seen any improvement in my life. I'm still without a job, still worried about the future. We still don't have decent schools. My kids still don't have health insurance. Maybe I should throw these guys out and give the Democrats a chance.*

We can't get to that place by just hoping it will happen. It'll take hard work, and that means we have to be present, on the ground, making it happen. We need a much more widespread and pervasive presence in local contests for elected office.

We have to contest every seat, for every office, in every county of the United States.

Here we have to take another lesson from the Republicans. In 1994, Newt Gingrich tried not to leave a single House race uncontested. He put people in every single district he could, even if they had no chance of winning. Lo and behold, some huge surprises happened, and the year's "throw the bastards out" mentality worked in his favor. Some of those people he didn't think had a chance actually won.

Let's learn from this. From now on, we have to run a candidate in every single election, no matter how unlikely they are to win. We cannot let a single seat in Congress, a single school board vacancy, or a single county commissioner's seat go uncontested. We've got to stop looking at congressional districts in which 70 percent of the population votes Republican as lost causes. We've got to reach out to the 30 percent who do vote for us and ask them to help us get out more of the Democratic vote. Let's focus on getting their districts from voting 30 percent Democratic to 40 percent, and then 45 percent, and then 51 percent. It can't be done in one election cycle. So we have to think in terms of many cycles, because change is possible over time.

But—again—change doesn't come if you don't fight to make it happen. We've got to put more backbone into our fight.

We need party discipline.

The Republicans have been ahead of us on this point for years. They've clearly gone too far—driving out their moderates, their pro-choice, pro-women, pro-environment, pro–civil rights old-timers, radically revolutionizing their party (and our country) in the process. The way they did it was no less than a purge, sealed by Gingrich's overwhelming wins in 1994, aided by an electorate that was completely fed up with politics as usual. Even I remember thinking, after the 1994 midterm elections, that maybe the shake-up wasn't such a bad thing.

I, like the country, quickly learned otherwise.

Newt Gingrich is all but gone from politics now, but back then, for a brief moment, he was a kingmaker. After he was elected Speaker of the House, everyone bowed down to him. He was a celebrity. Even Republican governors kowtowed to him in a way that I had never seen before or since.

I didn't kowtow. I made headlines early in January 1995

when I blasted the Republicans for trying to scrap nutrition programs for children, pregnant women, and the elderly, wondering aloud whether Gingrich and the Republican governors playing along with him had been "smoking opium in the Speaker's office."

After that, we pretty much had to meet. So I went to Washington. Gingrich was very personable and really smart. But he had become so infected with the Washington power bug that he'd lost the ability to see himself as others saw him. He also had no insight whatsoever into the ways he was letting his insecurities—about his background, about being an outsider, about not fully belonging—take over. He did something that day that still makes me laugh. He brought me into his office and motioned me to a sofa that was about a foot off the ground. He sat down in a chair that was about three feet off the ground. Then he waved in a photographer to take a picture of us together. Which, as you can imagine, meant that the image kept for posterity showed this big, massive guy towering over little scrawny me. I chuckled to myself: *This is so Washington.*

When I say we need to learn a lesson from the ways the Republicans brought discipline to their party and soldered their majority, I don't by any stretch of the imagination mean that we should effect an out-and-out purge or force our members to hew to a party line on extreme issues. I don't mean that our party should put its own interests in regaining and retaining power above the interests of our electorate, as Gingrich's Republicans did. On the contrary: We need to be true to ourselves by being faithful to our electorate, which overwhelmingly supports and shares our party's moderate core beliefs.

However, we also need a way to enforce our members' adherence to these core beliefs. Democrats shouldn't be crossing party lines to help Republican ideology dominate, or breaking ranks to vote for measures like the Medicare prescription bill, an election-year piece of legislation that, as usual, had a nice title but gives away our money to Bush contributors like the drug industry and HMOs.

In the future, there need to be consequences for Democrats who do. For one thing, there is no reason not to pose primary challenges to Democratic incumbents who vote with the Republicans on critical Democratic priorities. When our own folks vote with Tom DeLay, it means that DeLay, who is not stupid, gets to go to congressional Republicans from moderate districts and tell them he doesn't need their vote to pass his right-wing bill because he has enough Democratic votes to win. The "moderate" Republicans can go home and tell their constituents that they "stood up against" Tom DeLay while keeping him in power by voting for him as leader and falling in line with him on not-so-high-profile pieces of legislation.

What I'm saying may appall some of my reformist supporters. They'll say it has the ring of strong-arm tactics. I'm not trying to purge points of view from Congress. I like the idea of an inclusive party. If our opponents were reasonable people who shared our basic core values about fairness and decency, I'd think that by all means, Democrats should have the freedom to vote with them if their consciences prodded them to do so. But our opponents in Congress are extremists. We're fighting now for the future of our country and the future of democracy. To vote with the Republicans is to let extremism get the upper hand. In the past, our party's own ideals about inclusiveness kept us from having the necessary tools to fight. We need to toughen up. We can't afford to be divided by members peeling off on issues that touch upon our deeply held beliefs. We don't need to march in lockstep on every vote. But on critical votes that touch on our key issues, Democrats cannot abandon our core values. The history of the twentieth century teaches that we must never compromise with extremists. George Santayana put it well: "Those who do not learn from history are doomed to repeat it."

Because I want to use some of the strategies of the right wing doesn't mean I want to use all their strategies. I don't want us to use divisiveness to win elections. We'll never appeal to people's conflicts and resentments about race and ethnicity and sexual orientation and gender the way the Republicans do. If we were to do that, we might as well let the right wing run the country, because we won't do a better job.

The Democrats are intrinsically built differently from the right wing. We're not a movement of the ideologically hard-core. That's why imposing some discipline on the party doesn't pose any risk to democracy or our particular Democratic principles. We will win, now and in the years to come, by appealing to the best in America: to people's sense of patriotism, of collective responsibility and community. I know it can be done.

After I exited the presidental race, progressive Democrats began working with me all across America to try to put into practice the principles I've outlined here. With the support of our new organization, Democracy for America, we hope to revive the Democratic Party through grassroots organizing and return the party to its mainstream roots by electing fiscally responsible, socially progressive candidates. We back candidates who support universal health insurance, a foreign policy that's consistent with our democratic values, early childhood education, and strong environmental policies. And who uphold such basic American values as equality, opportunity, and social justice.

In 2004, we had eight hundred people running for office around the country. They were mostly people who came to politics through the Dean for America organization and stayed involved after I was no longer a candidate. They ran for things like the local school board, for the state assembly, for election supervisor, for mayor, for the House of Representatives, right on up to the U.S. Senate. We backed three people running for county supervisor of elections in

Florida. We also backed a couple of people running for student-body president in major universities, because they're people who will probably end up getting into national politics.

Democracy for America provided them with funds. Through a partnership with 21st Century Democrats and the Progressive Majority, we taught them how to go door-to-door, what kind of campaign literature they ought to have, how to do grassroots politics, how to raise money, and how to win elections. We're still having meet-ups. Above all, we're trying to push the Democratic wing of the Democratic Party to think long-term, not short-term, so that it can rebuild real strength and take back the party. We don't have a firm ideological litmus test for candidates. They don't have to share the same positions on every single issue. In more conservative states like Texas, we'll support candidates who are progressive by Texas standards, even if they don't meet the standards of progressives in Washington State or Vermont. That's how it has to be if we're truly to be an organization driven from the bottom up and not commanded merely by the folks here in Burlington. But there is a bottom line: We're not interested in electing Democrats who are essentially Republicans. We're interested in changing the country, not just getting people into office with a "D-" after their name.

We campaigned for some people who we knew couldn't win. That's because we believe that if we want eventually to win everywhere, we have to support good candidates in conservative districts so they can spread the message.

One thing that Democracy for America doesn't do is spend a lot of money on overhead. We don't have a ton of staff people, and we're not all about who's who in our organization. We're determined not to be like a Washington political action committee, where tons of money gets eaten up by staff and tons of attention is soaked up by whoever's running the organization.

We're committed to remembering that we're about the grass roots—ordinary Americans at the local level who are running for office and taking power back into their own hands. We believe in them—because they really do have the power.

We can't do this alone.

The Democrats now have about two thirds of the infrastructure to successfully fight off the right-wing extremist threat. There are some successful members of the progressive business community who see the danger to America that the right-wingers pose and are willing to finance the rest of the infrastructure that we need: the media coordination efforts, the think tanks, and the leadership training institutions. But to use all this successfully, we first need the discipline to work together for a cause greater than ourselves. That cause is America—at least the dream and vision that was America, until the right-wingers hijacked us.

A recurrent laugh line used by hundreds of Democratic politicians at thousands of Jefferson-Jackson dinners all over America is the old Will Rogers saying: "I don't belong to any organized party, I'm a Democrat."

We'll just keep laughing at that line until we laugh ourselves and the American dream right into extinction. It's time to be disciplined, time to be organized, time to renew ourselves, time to reach out.

It's time to fight back.

★ 7 ★

We Have the Power

Being organized and empowering people is the first part of taking back the power to change the country and restore American democracy. But there are specific reforms we must make a very high priority before we can succeed.

We need to restore the balance between corporate power and the ballot box.

We need to restore the balance between corporate rights and citizens' rights.

We need to narrow the wealth gap to show people that capitalism works for them.

We need to always stand up against the politics of division and fear, whether we are progressive or conservative or in the middle.

We need political institutions that people can believe in.

And we need a media willing to perform their watchdog role and hold politicians accountable for telling the truth.

And a few more things:

We need campaign-finance reform.

It's the precondition to restoring democracy in America. The McCain-Feingold campaign-finance law of 2002, which eliminated soft-money contributions to political parties, was a start, but it still contains enough loopholes to drive a Mack truck or at least several million dollars through. We need to go a lot further.

If we truly want to take the power to influence elections away from corporations and give it back to ordinary Americans, we have to stop the corporations from being essential to politicians' campaigns. That means some form of public financing for campaigns. We need to limit individual contributions to $250 apiece, prohibit any form of bundling (i.e., no Bush "Rangers" or "Pioneers"), and match donations of up to $100 with public money. To qualify for public funding, a presidential candidate should have to raise a substantial number of small donations from all around the United States, as is true of the current qualifying system for public funding in presidential elections.

Sound expensive? It's really not. One proposal that's been outlined by some campaign-finance-reform advocates would provide public funding for all presidential, Senate, and House candidates at a cost of just six dollars per American. Furthermore, think of how expensive our present system is. You pay the salaries of more than ten thousand lobbyists when you buy drugs, cars, towels, food, or almost any other product. You pay again when the president and Congress pass bills that funnel hundreds of billions of your tax dollars to oil companies, pharmaceutical companies, insurance companies, and manufacturers that move their jobs offshore, to name a few of the campaign contributors who later cash in on legislation.

You pay a third time when programs you like—such as money to help pay for your kids to go to college or money to help pay for new infrastructure for your schools, roads, and local hospitals—get cut to pay for corporate subsidies and tax giveaways. When state and local governments lack adequate funds to pay for these things (as they now do, thanks to the Bush tax cuts), your property taxes, college tuition bills, and health-insurance premiums soar. Your property taxes are now subsidizing the world's largest oil companies instead of going back to your community to pay for the things your neighbors, your parents, and your kids need to live a better life.

Public financing of all presidential, senatorial, and congressional campaigns would be a lot less costly than this, both in dollar amounts and in terms of the damage being done to our most vital public institutions.

We need more corporate accountability.

We've gone too far in this country toward granting rights to corporations while eroding workers' rights. We've become enthralled with the idea of corporate personhood— that a corporation functions like a person and has the same kinds of rights a person does, such as the right to free speech or privacy. With their records protected but consumer information accessible to anyone with the ability to pay, corporations now have greater privacy rights than people do!

A corporation is not a person. It's a group of people doing various jobs with the shared goal of maximizing profit and delivering a product or a service. Corporations are inherently neither bad nor good—they are amoral, like the free market. Often, when they are well run and corporate leadership is farsighted, the effects of their success benefit their workers and the larger community. But the truth is, while they sometimes do good by doing well, there's no reason to assume that their interests are in line with those of the national community. In fact, as big corporations operate in many countries and with the ability to move jobs from country to country, they're depressing wage scales around the globe and extorting tax concessions from nations fearful of increasing job losses.

The nations of the World Trade Organization, particularly the United States, were so anxious to advance the cause of globalization over the past two decades that they neglected to figure out how to control the destructive behavior of giant multinational businesses ahead of time. I think the capitalist system is the most productive economic scheme ever invented, but as in everything else we invent, it requires balancing. If we want Americans—and people around the world—to continue to believe that capitalism works for them, then we have to make capitalism really *work for them*. We need to restore the proper balance of power between corporations and individuals. One way to do it is by making clear to CEOs that they are accountable not just to their shareholders but to the people of the United States and of other nations.

The trend toward privatization so strongly promoted by the Republicans—who have moved, over the years, to privatize everything from social services to prisons to policing in Iraq—is a step in the wrong direction. Privatization has not turned out to be an effective cost-saver or guarantor of efficiency, but it *is* a way of reducing accountability to the public. The marriage between our government and major corporations has happened without the necessary steps being taken to assure transparency. The deregulation of the energy industry without transparency or accountability brought us Enron and much higher electric bills. The privatization of much of our security duties in Iraq has left us with the spectacle of torture at Abu Ghraib and a general lack of control over how our nationals comport themselves at a time when the eyes of the entire world are on us without sympathy.

I don't believe that the government should run everything. I don't think for a moment that government ownership of industries is efficient or sensible. For example, if we end up with a single-payer system to ensure that every American has health insurance, I think much of it should remain in the private nonprofit sector. However, I also think that publicly held corporations must be made to see that they have obligations to members of the public if they perform public functions, or if they are being paid or subsidized by taxpayers.

Our country should reward corporations that do the right thing by our environment and by their workers, not just those that do well by our political parties. We should penalize—by, for example, withholding government contracts—corporations that discriminate against gays or lesbians or women or members of minority groups, or any American, for that matter. We should be selective in granting government contracts to companies that take proper care of their workers. It may seem like a radical idea to suggest that a company's main responsibility should be to its employees and to our country and not strictly to its shareholders. But the concept is not entirely new or foreign—it was a postwar American idea, and it would be a terrible tragedy if, in the future, we were to follow the right-wing line by destroying the sense of collective obligation that made us great. That sense of common purpose goes back to the Declaration of Independence.

We have to reempower labor.

The American labor movement has never recovered from the blows dealt it by the Reagan administration. But the general disempowerment of our labor force isn't the fault of only the Republicans. The Democrats have half turned their backs on working people as well.

The failure to include labor and environmental standards in our free-trade agreements undermines those agreements. A government's unwillingness to take the side of workers when corporate greed runs rampant undermines capitalism, because ordinary people don't perceive the system's long-term social benefit. Right now working people have virtually no protections against the driving forces of the marketplace. That's not just morally wrong—it's unhealthy for our economy and for us as a society.

Labor unions are not perfect, and more of them need to follow the course of such progressive unions as the Service Employees International Union and focus on helping the most vulnerable Americans (immigrants, members of minority groups, and low-wage workers) cope with issues like a living wage and decent health benefits. Some of our labor unions got way off course in the past. But their overall success in serving as a counterweight to industry protected our free-market system by forestalling some of the excesses of government regulation that we still see in parts of Europe.

Ardent capitalists need to recognize that the success of democratic capitalism depends on the success of labor unions. In the long run labor reforms—like card check, which makes it easier for unions to organize low-wage workers—and social reforms, like universal health insurance and the institution of a combination of benefits and pay that would guarantee workers a living wage—will make capitalism stronger.

We need to increase voter turnout.

The first issue we need to address if we're going to get out the vote at a level required by a truly participatory democracy is the lack of excitement many people feel for the candidates put forth by our parties. Right now, in primaries and in general elections where there's a third-party candidate, a fair number of voters feel forced to choose between the candidate they prefer and the candidate they think is viable. In the end, if they really want to defeat the opposition, they choose the candidate they think is most likely to do so, without enthusiasm and without much pride. As they often put it, they feel as if they're choosing the lesser of two evils. A population that feels like this is not going to be very motivated to vote.

One way to overcome this problem is by changing our voting system so that people can vote for candidates they believe in without risking the kind of outcome we saw in 2000 when third-party candidate Ralph Nader drew enough votes from Al Gore to ensure President Bush's Electoral College win. Other countries do this through a multi-party system that rules by coalition. We can do it in America by bringing in a new voting system that allows coalitions to be built *as you vote.* It's called instant runoff voting.

Instant runoff voting is a system in which you vote by ranking two or three candidates in order of preference. When the votes are tallied, if your top choice gets knocked out of the running, your vote reverts to your number two, and so on. It's like having a runoff election, only you don't need two elections to do it. This system, which has attracted the interest of a number of reform-minded people around the United States, is already in use in Europe and in city council elections in Cambridge, Massachusetts. It's been approved for use by voters in San Francisco.

By way of illustration: Had we used instant runoff voting in 2000, most Nader supporters would have gone to the polls and voted for Ralph Nader first and Al Gore second. Since Nader, in the three-way tally afterward, wouldn't have finished in one of the top two slots, Al Gore would have been the beneficiary of roughly 60 percent of his votes and would have been chosen as the next president of the United States. (Most of Pat Buchanan's votes most likely would have gone to President Bush.)

Instant runoff voting would be beneficial for our electoral process, because it would encourage candidates to hold a firm set of principles without worrying that their beliefs could make them unviable. It would allow people to vote for candidates they really want to elect, thereby increasing both enthusiasm and turnout.

Providing voters with political candidates who inspire and excite them is a first step. But it's not enough—not at a time when many voters believe that their votes *simply don't count.* The U.S. Supreme Court's Florida fiasco in 2000 undermined people's belief in voting on a national level. Since that time, nothing has been done to restore their faith. The $3.9 billion that Congress allocated in 2002 to help counties buy new voting systems that would make problematic matters like chads a thing of the past has been spent largely on electronic touch-screen voting systems. These systems have malfunctioned in California and Florida. They've been shown to have serious security flaws, fatal software bugs, and even, in some cases, blurry screens that make it difficult for voters to tell exactly which candidate they are voting for. Worst of all, these machines leave no paper trail, meaning that there is no possibility of auditing the results of elections, making recounts impossible. Nearly 31 percent of the electorate will vote using these machines this year—which means that up to one third of the votes may be incorrectly tallied during this election.[1]

This nonsense has gone on long enough. We need voting machines that work.

As voters in Ohio, California, and other states have begun to do, we need to demand a national voting system with a verifiable paper trail and machines that can't be programmed to give the wrong results, unbeknownst to the people administering the voting.

Of all the initiatives I could mention, the most vital by far is the most simple: people taking power into their own hands, standing up, speaking out, and showing up in large enough numbers to effect change. Public involvement and grass-roots activism—bringing reform to every level of the political food chain, from school board seats on up—that's how change will happen in America.

Voting is not enough.

Like most public officials, I've been to hundreds of schools and colleges over the years, exhorting young people to vote. I don't do that anymore. In my mind, voting gets you a D if you want to live in a healthy democracy. If you want an A, you have to vote. *And* you have to work in a campaign for a candidate for any office three hours a week. *And* you have to send your favorite candidate five or ten or fifty dollars. (Dean for America showed that many small donations can add up to $53 million pretty fast.) To get an A+, you have to run for office yourself. Run for the school board, county supervisor, state legislature, Congress. Run for student council or library trustee. If ordinary Americans like you don't run, people from the right wing or the Christian Coalition will. That's how we got where we are now.

If you want your country back, you have to take it back. Believe me—the right-wingers aren't going to be nice about giving it back.

We have a tendency to believe that history corrects itself—that if the political pendulum swings too far in any one direction, it will sooner or later swing back and settle somewhere in the middle, thanks to the basic solidity of our institutions and the commonsense decency of our people.

There's some historical truth to that, but it's not going to happen now simply because it's a historical trend. It will happen if people like you use their power—the power they have in themselves, and the power they get by being part of a community—to make change.

If we allow current Republican policies and leadership to continue without debate, dissent, or innovative Democratic alternatives, we will not see anything vaguely resembling positive change or democratic restoration for the foreseeable future. For at least another generation, we will not see anything resembling the America that so many of us know, and love, and miss.

Who can stop that from happening? You can. We all can. And only we can.

Politicians can't solve our problems for us.

One of the things wrong with our democracy right now is that people have been searching for someone to come along and unlock the door to a better future, make everyone feel better again, and heal what ails our country.

The truth is, that person is you, not me or any other politician or leader.

If our country's in trouble, it's not only because George Bush is an inept president and the Democrats haven't stood up to him. It's because we're always looking for someone to come along and *save us.* What I learned during the campaign is that the only way for people to find this kind of salvation is by *saving themselves.* By tapping into the power that's already inside them and figuring out how to use that power in the outside world.

What I witnessed really deserves to be described by the word "salvation." There truly is a spiritual component to it: a profound something good deep in the heart of the American people. It is an abiding decency and hope. A desire to make America work again and to restore our moral greatness. A deep-seated belief in equality and in the dignity of all people that, I have learned, transcends the labels that people give to their politics. It is a basic given among decent Americans everywhere.

I am a different person now from what I was before the campaign. I failed to win the presidency, but I am more hopeful about America than I ever was before. I know this country and I know Americans much better now. I've learned that Americans are much stronger, fairer, and more caring than their leaders are. There are plenty of good values at work in America, even if they are in short supply in Washington. There is a willingness to accept others, a desire to be lifted up and inspired. There is a humility, a sense of our fallibility and of our obligation to others. There is a deep love for the community America has become over the last two hundred years, and there is a determination to restore that America.

I've been profoundly touched by my experience of the last two years, and even more touched by the remarkable people, from Hawaii to South Carolina to Maine, who have taught me so much. We will always be a great people and a great nation if we never again forget that *we* have the power.

NOTES

CHAPTER ONE

1. In the early 1990s, Maine, Vermont, and Texas entered into a low-level nuclear waste compact—essentially to pool our low-level waste—the kind of stuff that's left over after you inject people with radioactive dye when they need bone scans and other procedures, the gowns and the shoe covers from nuclear reactors—not the kind of stuff that kills you but that can't be put in the local dump. Neither Maine nor Vermont produces much low-level nuclear waste, but Texas does, and it was in all of our interests to form a compact together because if you're not in a compact and you open a nuclear waste disposal site, any state can send you their stuff and you can't stop them. So Texas planned to open the site and we put in some money and then began the usual battles with counties and environmental groups. Bush gave me his word that he would not take the money if he couldn't find a site. And he didn't.

2. Dionne, E. J., Jr., *Stand Up Fight Back* (New York: Simon & Schuster, 2004), p. 41.

3. Lomartine, Paul, "GOP Sent T-Shirt Team of Dedicated Infiltrators," *Palm Beach Post*, December 1, 2000, p. 1A.

4. Greg Palast, in *The Best Democracy Money Can Buy* (New York: Plume, 2003, pp. 11–81), provides a detailed description of how the state of Florida hired a private firm to "scrub the voter rolls," removing black voters in the guise of eliminating felons.

5. Supreme Court chief justice William H. Rehnquist had the nerve this year to publish a book, *Centennial Crisis*, on the disputed election of 1876 and then to claim that there were no meaningful parallels between this story and the election recount fiasco of 2000.

6. Halbfinger, David M., "Across U.S., Redistricting as a Never-Ending Battle," *New York Times*, July 1, 2003, p. A1.

7. Lewis, Charles, *The Buying of the President 2004* (New York: Perennial, 2004), p. 56.

8. Seelye, Katharine Q., "Voting Machine Executive Retracts Endorsement," *New York Times*, May 6, 2004, p. A31.

9. See, among others, Foer, Joshua, "Enter Right, Exit Left," *New York Times*, May 23, 2004, Section 4, p. 11.

10. Wilgoren, Jody, and David Rosenbaum, "Defying Labels Left or Right, Dean's '04 Run Is Making Gains," *New York Times*, July 30, 2003, p. A1.

11. Fineman, Howard, "The Dean Dilemma," *Newsweek*, January 12, 2004.

12. Dowd, Maureen, "The Doctor Is Out," *New York Times*, January 15, 2004.

13. Foer, Franklin, "Oops!" *New Republic*, February 23, 2004, p. 18.

14. Cohn, Jonathan, "Good Doctor," *New Republic*, July 28–August 4, 2003, p. 20.

CHAPTER TWO

1. Stewart, Christopher S., "In Trying Times, Many Ways to Ask, Will You Hire Me?" *New York Times,* August 31, 2003, Section 10, p. 1.

2. According to the Economic Policy Institute. See Bivens, Matt, "The Job Drain," *The Nation,* September 29, 2003, p. 6.

3. See, among many others, Steffy, Loren, "As We Bloat with Debt, Enablers Egg Us On," *Houston Chronicle,* June 6, 2004, p. 1.

4. Mayer, Jeremy D., *Running on Race: Racial Politics in American Campaigns 1960–2000* (New York: Random House), pp. 114–15.

5. Krugman, Paul, "The Tax Cut Con," *New York Times Magazine,* September 14, 2003, p. 54.

6. Derber, Charles, *Corporate Nation* (New York: St. Martin's, 1998), p. 12.

7. Krugman, Paul, "For Richer," *New York Times Magazine,* October 20, 2002, p. 62.

8. Lewis, Charles, *The Buying of the President, 2000* (New York: Avon, 2000), p. 10.

9. Krugman, "For Richer."

10. Lewis, *The Buying of the President 2000,* p. 2.

11. From Theodore Roosevelt's "The New Nationalism" speech, 1910.

12. Glain, Stephen J., "Rebuilding Iraq: Halliburton Says Employees Got Kickbacks on Iraq Work," *Boston Globe,* January 24, 2004, p. A1.

13. Kaus, Mickey, *The End of Equality* (New York: Basic Books, 1992), pp. 5–6.

14. Clymer, Adam, "Bush and Texas Have Not Set High Priority on Health Care," *New York Times*, April 11, 2000, p. A1.

15. Phillips, Kevin, *American Dynasty* (New York: Viking, 2004), pp. 114–15.

CHAPTER THREE

1. Nathans, Aaron, "Living with It: Karl Armstrong Honors His Motives in an Extreme Time," *Capital Times*, August 23, 2000, p. 1A.

2. Radosh, Ronald, *Divided They Fell: The Demise of the Democratic Party 1964–1996* (New York: Free Press, 1996), p. 196.

3. Cited in Radosh, p. 215.

4. Warner, Judith, and Max Berley, *Newt Gingrich* (New York: New American Library, 1995), p. 119.

5. Warner and Berley, p. 163.

6. Congressional Budget Office estimate. See, among many sources, Stevenson, Richard W., "Still Uncertain, Budget Surplus Is Gobbled Up," *New York Times*, May 27, 2001, p. 1.

7. Thirty-four percent, according to Juan Williams's "Bush Shouldn't Write Off the Black Vote," *The New York Times*, June 16, 2004. Williams also notes that President Bush, whose immigration policies have been roundly censured by advocates for immigrants and particularly Latinos, currently enjoys the support of a third of the Hispanic popular vote, according to a poll by Zogby International.

8. Dionne, E. J., Jr., *Stand Up Fight Back* (New York: Simon & Schuster, 2004), p. 92.

CHAPTER FOUR

1. Kelly, Michael, "Saint Hillary," *New York Times Magazine*, May 23, 1983, p. 22.
2. Cited in Steinfels, Peter, "Beliefs," *New York Times*, May 29, 1993, Section 1, p. 25.
3. For the Saint Hillary debate, see Nussbaum, Bruce, "What Does the 'Politics of Meaning' Mean for America?" *Business Week*, June 21, 1993, p. 38; "The Politics of Meaning: Round-table Discussion," *Tikkun*, September 1993, p. 19; Podolsky, J. D., "The Thinker," *People*, September 20, 1993, p. 89.
4. According to a 2003 Pew poll, 62 percent of Americans like the way President Bush frequently invokes his religious faith in his public statements, and 11 percent think he doesn't speak of it often enough. Poll cited in Foer, Franklin, "Beyond Belief," *New Republic*, December 29, 2003–January 12, 2004, p. 22.
5. Brock, David, *The Republican Noise Machine: Right-Wing Media and How It Corrupts Democracy* (New York: Crown, 2004).
6. Warner, Judith, and Max Berley, *Newt Gingrich: Speaker to America* (New York: New American Library, 1995), pp. 155–56.
7. Brock, *The Republican Noise Machine*, p. 250.
8. Staples, Brent, "Americans Have a Cool Debate About a Hot-Button Topic," *New York Times*, March 2, 2003, Section 4, p. 12.

CHAPTER FIVE

1. Tumulty, Karen, "Inside the Mind of Howard Dean," *Time*, January 12, 1994, p. 24.
2. Schweitzer, Sarah, and Tasha Robertson, "A Back Condition Wins Dean a Vietnam-Era Draft Deferment," *Boston Globe*, September 21, 2003, p. B9.
3. Lyman, Rick, and Christopher Drew, "33 Years Later, Draft Becomes Topic for Dean," *New York Times*, November 22, 2003, p. A1.
4. VandeHei, Jim, and William Branigin, "Brother's Remains Found in Laos, Dean Says," *Washington Post*, November 19, 2003, p. A9.
5. Tumulty, Karen, "The Dems Get Ready for Prime Time," Time.com, April 28, 2003.
6. Mooney, Brian C., "Democratic Party Plans Timely Ad Campaign," *Boston Globe*, December 14, 2003, p. A4.
7. Brownstein, Ronald, "Democratic Hopefuls Rally Behind Bush," *Los Angeles Times*, March 21, 2003, Part 1, p. 20.
8. Pickler, Nedra, "Dean to Slow Criticism of Bush Amid War," Associated Press, March 20, 2003.
9. VandeHei, Jim, "Dean Invites More Scrutiny by Switching Key Stances," *Washington Post*, August 30, 2003, p. A1.
10. "Misperceptions, the Media, and the Iraq War," PIPA/Knowledge Networks Poll: The American Public on International Issues, October 2, 2003.

CHAPTER SIX

1. Kirkpatrick, David, "Some Big Conservative Donors, Unhappy with Bush, Say They Won't Back His Campaign," *New York Times*, June 4, 2004, p. A23.
2. Carpenter, Traci E., "I Cannot Be Charted," *Newsweek*, July 12, 2004.

CHAPTER SEVEN

1. Ladendorf, Kirk, "Security Debate Slows Electronic Voting," Cox News Service, June 14, 2004.